The Game Audio Director's Guide

The Game Audio Director's Guide explores the Audio Director's role in video game production, showing how responsibilities change across different project phases and production demands.

This book gives aspiring and current Audio Directors practical frameworks, roadmaps, and models to tackle the challenges of game audio leadership. You'll learn how to transition between projects, manage teams, balance creative and technical work, and understand how audio direction evolves throughout a game's development. Using industry examples and real-world insights, this book helps you move from hands-on sound work to strategic leadership, so you can shape the overall audio vision while adapting to each production phase.

This book is essential for audio professionals moving into or already working as Audio Directors in the video game industry. It's also valuable for game audio designers wanting to understand leadership; students studying game audio or sound design; and educators teaching game development, interactive media, or audio production.

Rob Bridgett is a British-Canadian Audio Director who has worked in video game audio development since 2000 (Vivendi Universal, Activision, Square Enix, PlayStation). Rob is the author of seven books about game audio development, including *Leading with Sound* (2021), *Working with Sound* (2023), and *Sound Principles* (2024).

The Game Audio Director's Guide

Rob Bridgett

Routledge
Taylor & Francis Group
LONDON AND NEW YORK

First published 2027
by Routledge
4 Park Square, Milton Park, Abingdon, Oxon OX14 4RN

and by Routledge
605 Third Avenue, New York, NY 10158

Routledge is an imprint of the Taylor & Francis Group, an informa business

For Product Safety Concerns and Information please contact our EU representative GPSR@taylorandfrancis.com. Taylor & Francis Verlag GmbH, Kaufingerstraße 24, 80331 München, Germany.

British Library Cataloguing-in-Publication Data
A catalogue record for this book is available from the British Library

ISBN: 9781041258926 (hbk)
ISBN: 9781041258919 (pbk)
ISBN: 9781003748465 (ebk)

DOI: 10.4324/9781003748465

Typeset in Times New Roman
by codeMantra

As a settler, I respectfully acknowledge the island of K'taqmkuk (Newfoundland) on which this book was written, and on which I work and listen, as the unceded ancestral homelands of the Mi'kmaq and Beothuk.

Contents

Introduction

May 2015.

I am sitting in the middle of a crowded, bustling open-plan office space, surrounded by the dev team, all working on various things, some of them finishing up one game, while others are working on prototypes, playbooks, and sandboxes for a new game. I am skimming through a document on my screen and, fresh from having one of my initial meetings with my new creative director, I am somewhere between mild confusion and disorientation with a familiar sense of background anxiety.

I'm perhaps two weeks into my new role at Eidos Montreal; I've moved out here to Montreal ahead of my family joining me, temporarily living out of a self-catering hotel room a few blocks from the studio. There is a lot going on. But at this moment, I am fixated on one thing. I'm following a feeling, an image, a sound world starting to form in my mind. The prior meeting with our creative director was to talk about the music of the game we are starting to make, what was to become *Shadow of the Tomb Raider*. I have listened to him talk for about three hours and have somehow come away with a glimpse of this sound world in my head. I can describe it now as a dense jungle, filled with the sounds of exotic birds, but it is heard from a dangerous, frightening perspective, it is a sound that feels alien to me, more like another planet, then there is this tone, this mood, it is perhaps the music. These could be traditional wind instruments, such as flutes, but it is not what we are used to hearing, and it is a much slower, more natural sound, completely fitting in with the rest of the sounds of the birds and insects I can imagine – it is a bit like humid air itself, like the beams of light shining through the water vapour in the air.

At some point someone taps me on the shoulder, and we head off for coffee to discuss other immediate practicalities, but the vision I have just experienced is very strong, I can recall it at will, and it is now an actual place that I can go to and revisit in my mind.

A few days afterwards, I am meeting with a potential composer for the project in a local coffee shop, our first meeting. We get along very well, and as I start to describe the vision, the sounds of the coffee shop around us seem to disappear and we are both now in this imagined jungle world. As I continue to

DOI: 10.4324/9781003748465-1

describe and explain what we can hear and feel, like the mood, the temperature, or the light, I mention the birds, the jungle, the humidity, then the instruments and the stretched-out tonal feeling, but also that these sounds are a part of the jungle, not really a score, they are coming from somewhere diegetic in that world. His eyes widen, and he's very clearly also spent time imagining and exploring a world in which pre-Columbian cultures continued to thrive and produce music and culture… we leave the coffee shop and I go about the rest of my day. The next morning, I see an email from Brian D'Oliveira (the composer in question) who had been working all through the night on sketches of music, I open the file attachments and it is what I imagined, only it is far more; it has detail, a shape, and cultural presence in the performance that feels like I am actually hearing something that is seeping through an opening in time and space. There are wind instruments and percussion sounds that feel ancient, yet familiar, and phrased in new ways I've never heard before, this brings even more of my imagined world into focus and into reality. Incredible. I excitedly begin to play the files to other directors on my team as well as the sound team, who all respond excitedly, though I do recall our producer at the time being a little less fever-dream excited and more practical in terms of getting some competing bids first before we commit to anything. The big moment was playing this for our creative director, I had assembled some of Brian's demos to fit alongside concept images of the jungle environment, mixed in with some authentic Peruvian Amazon ambience recordings. We went into the review theatre to listen together. There was a lot of uncomfortable silence as I played the files, nobody said anything as the music played from what I remember. The one-minute excerpt seemed to last for about five minutes as we both sat there listening. Then at the end, the lights came up and Dan, our creative director, walked over and simply hugged me – he said it is the first time he could see the game that he had in his head, the first time he could feel like being there in that world – and the first time he felt that it was a real thing that we could now go and make. We did already have a lot of concept art and prototypes at this point, but what he meant was that for him, as a visionary and a director, it was the first time this world in his head actually felt like an achievable reality we could put onscreen as a team and that a player could explore and be inside… we now had the beginnings of a map of how to get there, and we also knew how to recognize it when we arrived.

1 Direction and Vision

This is a book about visions and the process of directing those visions. It is also about trying to do that while being in a dynamic environment where everything changes over time, which can be a bit of a problem as we generally like things to feel stable and in control, especially as directors. One of the main problems with this is that nobody tells you how dynamic it can be, and everyone you meet seems to talk in concrete terms about what is happening, why, when and with whom. Being able to envision something that is resolute while at the same time open to the idea that at any moment it can change, is the central magic trick of both direction (in any discipline) and of confidence (the magic trick of confidence is always the *appearance* of confidence).

In this book we'll dive into some of the overall shapes and contexts of audio direction over the last 25 years in the video games industry. Project by project, studio by studio, things evolve and change… however, overall the silhouette of audio direction for games remains mostly the same. Most problems with understanding direction seem to stem from the low-level details becoming more important than the big picture… for instance how a certain kind of motorcycle engine needs to be recorded near a lake in the desert, or how a specific kind of microphone must be used to capture the signature sound layer triggered for an iconic final boss attack. That's the double-edged sword at play here, that all those juicy, exciting details of 'how' can obscure the big picture of 'why'. As sound designers, audio programmers, dialogue designers, composers (music designers), or interactive mixers, we seem all too happy to give away the recipes and ingredients of our magic tricks, yet as directors, we're less inclined to reveal what's going on underneath. Perhaps the magic tricks of direction aren't ones we're prepared to expose because they reveal too much, or too little?

Over the last seven years, I've had the opportunity of coaching new audio directors taking on the role for the first time. And while every person is different, their backgrounds, their teams and projects reflecting different entertainment experiences, it is through this work that there has emerged a clearer view for me of the general overall 'territory of responsibility' of what the audio director role entails and what areas a director needs to take

DOI: 10.4324/9781003748465-2

immediate ownership of in order to gain (and remain in) control of the audio on a project. There are also some common, relatable orientation concepts that establish which way is up, as well as identity problems that can be resolved along the way.

This reflection on what we all might assume to be basic knowledge feels increasingly necessary, as responsibilities become ever-more undefined, pressure is higher to do more with less, and in most cases our traditional hands-on skills that have served us so well during our time in the trenches, seem to exert influence over our perception of what audio direction is – seeming in most cases to imply a continuation of all the previous practical hands-on work with the *addition* of more responsibilities at the director level. The opposite tends to be the case, as the hands-on work of sound design falls away to make room for new priorities of fully understanding the project. A new audio director may suddenly find themselves doing no sound design or implementation at all, and instead helping guide the team, and the game itself, to solve wider problems. This transition can be daunting, and a homesickness for sound design, composition or integration can be a powerful feeling.

That the role is ambiguous to such a high degree will come as no surprise. Game development in general forgoes fixed industrial structures and role definitions, instead favouring what works at a particular studio, for a particular group of personalities, on a particular project at a particular production phase.

The role of audio director taken across the industry as a whole is mostly incoherent. What one director confidently declares to be the de facto, indisputable concrete responsibilities of the role are completely different from what the next director considers to be the essentials… and you'll hear this from directors who work in the *same studio* on different projects. When you pull the camera back to include other directors at different studios and publishers, the differences can become even more marked, and it all seems to come down to studio culture, personality, personal style, and in many cases, occupying a small niche that each director has created for themselves. Some directors appear to be doing the work of audio leads, composers, programmers, designers, and integrators, in the guise of a director. When a director is essentially directing their own content work in this way, is the direction guiding the work, or is the work guiding the direction?

And yet, when we look over at the adjacent disciplines, at Art Directors, Design Directors, and User Experience Directors, we tend to see far more direction and far less (if any) authoring of the hands-on content.

It became evident through my coaching and conversations with directors – that there are many areas an audio director needs to let go of, the bits that audio direction *isn't,* areas of work and responsibility that should be entrusted to the audio team itself. To some, these hands-on areas seem to be psychological constructions necessary to personal identity, whether that be directing actors in the booth, field recording, sound design and implementation, composing, or even audio programming. Regardless of the project, these were areas where the director was unconsciously using the notion of direction and approval-control in order to open up space and time for them to do their own thing. For me, this forms the initial work of any coaching context – to find out what are the unconscious redlines and work areas they are protecting, unable to let go of, because they have become welded to their previous identities as sound designers, programmers or composers. This sense of over-stretching and over-ownership is a common thematic problem among audio directors who are under high pressure, and it gives us an opportunity to dig into why.

People often assume the role of a director is to talk, but at first it is to listen; to the team, to the culture. A spirit of openness is a key to co-creativity, leading eventually to clarity and understanding. Clarity is very much a strategic advantage when the environment all around is noisy, and *especially* when pressure is high.

Strategy is also an extremely important area of focus for a director. Audio teams today are no longer the static fixed group of six or seven full-time studio-based employees – a team is now a mosaic. Teams dynamically grow and shrink to meet the upcoming waves of production needs. Audio teams today can consist of contractors, outsourced specialists, co-dev generalists, perhaps an army of central audio craft experts, as well as the core dev-studio audio team members. This mosaic approach requires new ways of working that are at once near-, mid- and far-sighted, strategic and reflective. Which is why having an audio director who is busying themselves in the weeds and details of 'how', scrambling to make content for an ever-changing upstream dependency, represents an increasingly high-risk profile for a development team heading into the series of tsunami waves of upcoming production. Finding the time and space to think strategically should be prioritized at the director's level, you will have access to information and overall planning that enables you to use audio to achieve the project's goals; rather than unknowingly working against them.

All this leads us to some fundamental questions. What is the identity of an audio director? Are they audio, are they game development, are they leadership? Are they a blend to varying degrees of all three, leaning into and out of these identities at different times? Is identity as a director fixed or dynamic? When exploring these questions, through the needs of projects and teams, they each open up new working areas and opportunities that can be surprising.

For example, an audio director who is tasked with the higher levels of delivering the creative vision can quickly find themselves, their direction and language, overlapping the same territories as the creative director – where the same communication skills and thinking can be just as effectively applied across all disciplines, not just audio. So, there is opportunity for such a director to play a wider role on the project. At the same time, remaining centred on audio, and its four branches of dialogue, music, sound design, and mix, can lead to compromises where we often wish we were able to have more influence over areas outside of sound – so there are a lot of choices to make.

An audio director who is able to de-couple direction from hands-on design and implementation often solves two immediate problems for the team and the project – giving the director a huge amount of content and work to direct and provide notes on keeps them out of the weeds, while also ensuring the team has the answers they need to succeed and grow in their work *and* giving the team autonomy and ownership over the design and integration of sound. Separating the feedback from the work itself feels like a critical point here, getting the perspective of someone whose hands have not touched the sounds or the engine removes bias colouring from decision-making. As a director, you will quickly find you need to evaluate and provide notes on not just how the game sounds, but on the context around what is happening onscreen, and how it feels. How things *feel* is perhaps a more useful way in which to direct, leaving room for different design solutions to come forwards. Again, this form of direction also ensures clarity for the autonomy of the team to figure out how to make it feel the way that is needed. As a director, I am accountable for the brief. As a sound team, you are responsible for executing and delivering on that brief.

This first stage in this whole process of looking at direction is often a basic identity and responsibility audit that clears the path for an audio director to be able to focus on 'direction'. Any team asking or expecting their audio director to *also* be hands-on in the engine needs to understand the temporary nature of these possibilities as scale and pressure increases along the production timeline.

Hands-on content creation *and* direction seem to be only possible with a *very* small team size, project scope or culture (where other directors in adjacent disciplines are also hands-on, and, most importantly, are successful at it). As soon as the scale of work becomes such that direction and implementation take away from the time and focus needed for each other, this prevents the audio director from doing both effectively – put simply, both direction and the hands-on work are now being done poorly.

Many audio directors today, entered the industry onto projects at a time where the scale was reasonable enough to have a hand in everything, and they became used to the level of control possible at that scale. As project scope and team sizes have exploded, that same degree of coverage is simply not possible at the same level. Letting go of the idea of full control and authorship can be a relief, and anywhere I see this struggle, remediation of this entanglement is where the conversation is centred.

2 Design

Another point of discovery in conversations with sound people of every level of seniority is in dispelling the idea that sound for games is an artistic practice. While games themselves may be considered an art form, in every bit the same way cinema is, sound for games, in all its branches, is very much a creative *design* discipline. Any sound effect, dialogue line, music cue of any kind must fulfil a brief, and more broadly, for the overall architectural experience of sound in games the *mix* of all the elements must also fulfil an overall brief for the player.

This is not to say that a design brief fulfilled cannot be aesthetic; in fact, one of the more exciting things about design of all kinds is the way it is able to simultaneously fulfil a brief and be at once functional and aesthetic.

As an example, outside of video game development, and to paraphrase Kevin McCloud, Architecture (as one of the main design disciplines) is a pragmatic discipline, involving layout and organization, and of course it should also speak of beauty and delight. Yet it has an important function to keep us warm and dry. Art doesn't have any of these constraints. Art doesn't have to solve any problems. Art's purpose? It doesn't need one. Design does have a purpose; it must fulfil the brief. Its primary function is to solve a problem. It is also highly interdependent on other disciplines and craftspeople to achieve the needs of any brief, so collaboration is crucial.

The point here is that sound for games is not a sensible outlet for your personal expression or feelings, and I would encourage you to move away from any starting point that considers game sound as an art form for individual self-expression and creative self-actualization in that sense. The creative act can sometimes *feel* like we are creating art, and *feel* like self-expression, yet the moment we get notes and feedback and begin to iterate, we cross back into the reality that we are fulfilling a design brief. Perhaps this is why a great many audio people can struggle with receiving notes and feedback on their work. Game development is a fundamentally collaborative design-driven, *co-creative* act between a team of many different backgrounds, disciplines and experiences. Any artistic impulse here is a collective and shared one, so removing yourself from being at the centre of the work is important; the

DOI: 10.4324/9781003748465-3

work is at the centre, not you. While a sound designer or composer may be somewhere on their journey in understanding this differentiation, a director *must* fully understand this distinction as *the brief* and its execution are central to the process of direction. One of many potential definitions of the practical realities of a director I propose here is 'Working as part of a team to execute a brief'.

The needs of teams hiring entry- or mid-level audio professionals are clearly targeted at their ability to be hands-on. The ability to design and implement sounds and sound systems at high speed – with reliable design, technical and implementation skills. As those talents and the confidence that come with them eventually grow, it is at the ownership and leadership level that career progression becomes possible. New senior sound designers can often find themselves in emergent leadership positions, and can become frustrated by the many human and political elements of this work, as well as the endless micro-negotiations that are present in those deeper collaborative waters. These are responsibilities where audio skills, audio thinking and audio knowledge, in general, are no longer the most prominent features of achieving a good result for the team and the game.

Many sound designers, to be fair, have no desire to leave behind the craft part of the sound work completely, and would prefer to stay hands-on as senior or principal sound designers, rather than become the leaders, or representatives for audio on teams and projects. However, the upwards gravity-pull of the career hierarchy and with it the potential for increasing salaries within company structures exerts real pressure here. This leads to the ambiguous idea that sound leadership can also include the continued implementation and design work of sound, which leads to conflict in terms of focus and responsibility. To some degree this absolutely makes sense. The more a leader knows of the day-to-day hands-on world of design and implementation, surely the better they can lead a team who works in this world? Engineering, for example has quite similar pathways here, where coding knowledge is essential to be able to manage and direct teams of coders and to help optimize their work. However, at some point in the ascension up the ladder of responsibilities, there is a tipping point, in terms of direction at least, where rather than the coaching and optimization focus that might come from and be expected from a lead or a supervisor, the *director's* focus moves from what is going on underneath the hood, behind the scenes, to what is going on at the top layer, the layer where interaction between the player and the game takes place – and it is on this level that knowledge of the hands-on under-the-hood world of optimization, memory management, dynamic systems, falls away… instead, with direction, we have an area where knowledge of the happenings under-the-hood confuse and complicate the direction itself, leading to compromises that are not based on what the player is experiencing. The focus for onscreen direction moves entirely away from the way the sounds are made and integrated to the way the sounds are experienced by the audience. And it is from here where the director must drive and lead the team. *Onscreen is the only truth,* as my old creative director used to tell our entire discipline-director's team. This is where all our work would either live or die. An example I often cite: it doesn't matter how clever or complex your reverb systems are, if they are doing ground-breaking ray-tracing piggybacking on other subsystems to dynamically adjust the reflections based on every wall and surface material, and adapting to the volumetric dimensions of every space dynamically without having to manually make a single reverb box, if there is no need to hear reverb in the game and its presence is muddying up the mix and reducing clarity… get rid of the reverb. Having clarity of the experience, what is important for the player to hear, (and when) is the most important thing. I will propose another important definition of direction here as 'Onscreen is the only truth. Ask: What is the most important thing for the player to hear?'

Of course, a director can have a far more profound impact on technical optimization for the team by understanding the clarity of the experience, and being able to remove or de-prioritize unnecessary features – removing those complicated reverb systems may save your team literally years of wasted work and millions of dollars in effort, simply by realizing that those solutions are not necessary to the particular experience your team is actually making. Sure, they may have some small incremental impact on what the player hears and feels in some small areas of the game, but if it is not noticeable enough, or core to the experience, then it must be deprioritized. Clarity is an evolved species of optimization, and at the director's level: clarity is optimization.

Most of the complexity and turmoil, it seems, comes from ambiguity between the leadership roles of lead or supervisor, where hands-on understanding of the work is critically important for the team, and areas where direction is required, which demands the surrender of knowledge of what is happening underneath the surface of the experience, and instead is about what the player experiences, touches, sees, hears, and feels. This is where things can get messy. It is the tipping point between lead/supervisor and director where perspectives on the work, and how it is reviewed, completely change. A lead, in an ideal world, would be completely dedicated to the experience under the hood, in the engine, and at the asset level – whereas a director would be completely dedicated to the top-level onscreen world of what the player sees, feels and hears. Once you clear that hill, you are in a completely different territory where what goes on under the hood will not help you one bit in solving the creative issues of the game experience. In fact, the more you know of what goes on underneath, the less effective it could be argued you are as a director of the onscreen experience, as your focus and influence is elsewhere, not on the onscreen experience. Similarly, as a lead, if you're focussed on the onscreen experience, you are likely to be compromising the integrity of the systems and content designs that are at work, along with all their triggering logic (Figure 2.1).

Once in that ambiguous territory, you need to ask fundamental questions to find your priorities and your heading. In essence, audio direction means

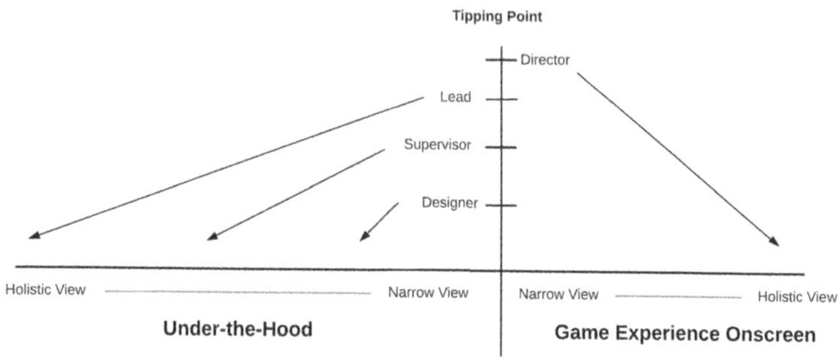

Figure 2.1 Passing the tipping point from audio lead to direction

leaving behind the relative safety and mastery over your chosen field of audio design and becoming instead an expert in the project. Knowing its characters, its story, its motivations and aspirations, its pillars, and its business model. This new expertise and inside-out knowledge can be traversed, explored and amplified in unique ways by a person who understands what this means in terms of sound – what does the game sound like, why must it sound this way, what is it important for this game to communicate to the player? Almost certainly, this perspective will hinge on the understanding of what the game must *feel* like. As part of this process of knowing your project, your audio identity becomes a secondary aspect, yet an essential lens through which you will understand the game and the business being built around that game.

We're not abandoning sound thinking. Audio sensitivity can help identify unseen problems and pitfalls with any design, and it is necessary that you are there to answer and be an ambassador *for* audio and the audio team, but audio is never more important than the game itself. Great care is needed in messaging, communication and behaviour. Attitudes that display this sense of siloed 'audio entitlement' (embodied by the oft-weaponized 'but, sound is 50% of the experience' phrase), can be counter-productive in a collaborative situation like game development. Instead of improving the collaborative conditions needed for good audio, pushing for the most important billing will always increase animosity towards audio and will close down collaborative opportunities. Audio can easily become perceived as a wounded craft that sees itself as aggrieved and elevated above the other crafts of game development. Closer collaboration is the desired outcome, and nobody wants to work with an audio team that thinks, acts and talks as though it is the greater part of the game experience than all the other parts.

So, somewhere mixed-up in-between all of these worlds of strategy, politics, identity, communication, perception and, culture is the intuitive understanding of what an audio director is and isn't, responsible for. On this front, things often get messy and confusing right from the beginning.

3 Decoding the Job Description

So where does it all begin?

The seeds for confusion tend to be sewn early, in the attempts to express and describe the role of an audio director. By looking at job descriptions of audio directors, we can find clues as to where this begins. Funnily enough, many job descriptions for sound designer and senior sound designers also include almost all of the same needs as those being asked for in terms of directors or leads.

The job description feels like a symptom of audio stereotypes … granted, as I am discovering while writing this book, attempting to describe the role of an audio director and list their responsibilities is somewhat attempting the impossible, and at the same time in danger of playing into assumptions and cliches.

The main issue with a job description seems to be that by specifying virtually everything that is the possible work of 'audio' across the project, it fails to distil *accountability* for audio, instead spraying endless lists of the responsibilities of audio onto the page, perhaps hoping that they can find someone who can 'do it all' and still be accountable.

Whenever an audio team is looking for someone to lead them, they often assume that what they are looking for is someone who can do *all* the things that a sound designer and integrator can do, *plus* all the management, direction, communication, and planning, *plus* be responsible for running the physical studio spaces themselves, *plus* designing and literally building (in some job ads I have seen) new studio spaces, directing actors, the list goes on. I don't think I've ever read a job ad looking for an audio director which simply states '*what we are looking for is someone to look after the vision of the project and the team from an audio perspective*'. Now, of course, the whole world may be encompassed in that description, but it leaves the details until later and it makes clear the overriding priority is accountability for audio.

Audio seems, though to have found a special place where expectations span both hands-on and hands-off worlds. Let's compare and contrast an example… two jobs, both at a triple-A studio, listed at the same time, right

DOI: 10.4324/9781003748465-4

next to one another, on the same team. I've added in brackets after each line item to whom I think the responsibility really belongs.

Audio Director

- Contribute meaningful content that inspires the team – It's expected that you will balance both content creation and managerial work (Individual Contributor + Manager).
- Implement sound content with native tools (IC).
- Manage audio team deliverables against development timelines (Production).
- Identify and prioritize tech needs (Production/Lead).
- Review and provide feedback on team contributions (Director).
- Foster career growth and educational development of team members (Manager).
- Work with leadership to identify long-term visions for the company (Director).

Art Director

- Be highly creative; Imagine and communicate vision to leadership and the team to develop new content that players will love (Director).
- Collaborate with multiple teams, including Design, Programming, and Production to develop world-class player experiences and interpret the needs of all development disciplines into final artwork (Director).
- Deliver effective feedback across all art disciplines – concept, modelling, environment, tech art, lighting,Visual Effects, etc. (Director).
- Collaborate with the teams to identify great ideas and steer them through the pipeline (Director).
- Filter multiple sources of analysis and feedback into visual direction for creating new art (Director).
- Think strategically about art and how it informs the player experience (Director).
- Work within the style of our projects with an eye towards driving the brand forward (Director).

It is an eye-opener. As mentioned, I have placed, in brackets, the role to which each requirement is usually attributed, whether that is director, lead, IC (Individual Contributor, such as a sound designer or implementer), manager or producer. There are *two* director-level accountability areas listed for the audio job, and every area listed is director-level for the art job.

The description for the art director role is wonderfully illustrative of what we are missing from the audio side. We see the work of *actual direction* being described – we see the *Why* being addressed. Vision, collaboration and *interpretation* (beautiful!) of the requirements of the other disciplines, delivering feedback across a multitude of art sub-disciplines, '*steering* of ideas' (I love this!) through the pipeline (note: *not* the actual implementation of ideas into the pipeline with your own hands... but steering!) – responding to analysis and feedback from multiple sources, strategy and philosophy, even further... brand ownership and development.

We should read more Art Director job descriptions; they give examples of what areas an audio director should also be expected to achieve on a project. Given the two example descriptions above, I'd be excited to jump into the art role and immediately start having an impact. Conversely, for the audio director description, it just feels like I'd be walking some impossible tightrope of trying to please everyone, scrambling to stay afloat, a stressed-out dogsbody whose head is spinning in so many directions they cannot centre and understand the work. This will likely suit someone who is aggressively trying to *own* everything, and not allowing others on the team to have autonomy and ownership over areas like integration. My issue here is really with the expectation of implementation. Implementation is a massively complex and detailed area of responsibility which demands *full attention*, and especially so at the highest quality bars of our industry. It is not an area you can just have a go at and do good-enough work. Putting an audio director on implementation is a disservice to both the craft of sound integration, and to the work and focus of direction – you'll get both done poorly. The notion that an audio director could use a small portion of their time to do this work to the level of a seasoned senior or principal sound designer is deeply concerning.

To me, the audio director job overall shown here describes an Audio Lead with additional accountability, while the art director position is a high-level directorial role – an *actual* director. This description is looking for someone who can handle the *How* and the *Who* of the project. Presumably the actual audio vision is being supplied elsewhere, probably by the art director.

Reading these two descriptions, the Art Director most resonates, because when I read that description, I see actual direction very well articulated and it is clear what I would have to do. What the Audio Director description tells me is that the team is really seeking an Audio Lead, and that direction is a secondary or tertiary concern here to content design and integration. It also tells me a lot about the attitudes and environment in which the audio work is expected to happen.

4 You Arrive in the Director's Seat – Now What?

No project is simple. Every one is stressful. You're in the director's seat. Whether this is your first Audio Director (AD) job, or whether you have landed at a new company and project from a different team, your initial imprints of the project and team are going to be similar. What is the game about? Who are the key people on the team who have this knowledge? What am I *actually* responsible for? You will discover this through listening and asking questions, but it is ultimately going to be up to you to find this out and put some definitions in place to be clear about this. It is time to forget the job ad that said you'd be doing everything, because you will in fact only need to be doing very specific things, or at least your top priorities will be sitting across specific areas. While doing that, you will also pick up on the tone and culture of the team, their rituals, how they interact with one another, what is the energy level like, the *environment* in which the work will happen. The good news is that you will be drinking all this in, mostly consciously, but also subconsciously, and as you start to work and begin to collaborate, and the shape of the game you are making, who you are making it with, and all its challenges, will unfold.

'Wayfaring'

As you likely have already discovered, the path of developing a game is never a direct line to the finished product. In Tim Ingold's book, *Lines: A Brief History*, we can find some useful analogies for thinking about game development. Ingold describes the process of acquiring experience of a place by participating in it – by 'laying a trail of life, contributing to its weave and texture'. He describes this as wayfaring; a way of knowing that is opposite to formal education, a process of acquiring skills and gathering knowledge through movement, immersion and lived experience.

This feels to me every bit how game development works; theory gets you only so far, you have to make a mark onscreen and respond to it. For audio, you can never know how to make sound for a particular game, on a particular team, until you are participating directly in its development and learning its

DOI: 10.4324/9781003748465-5

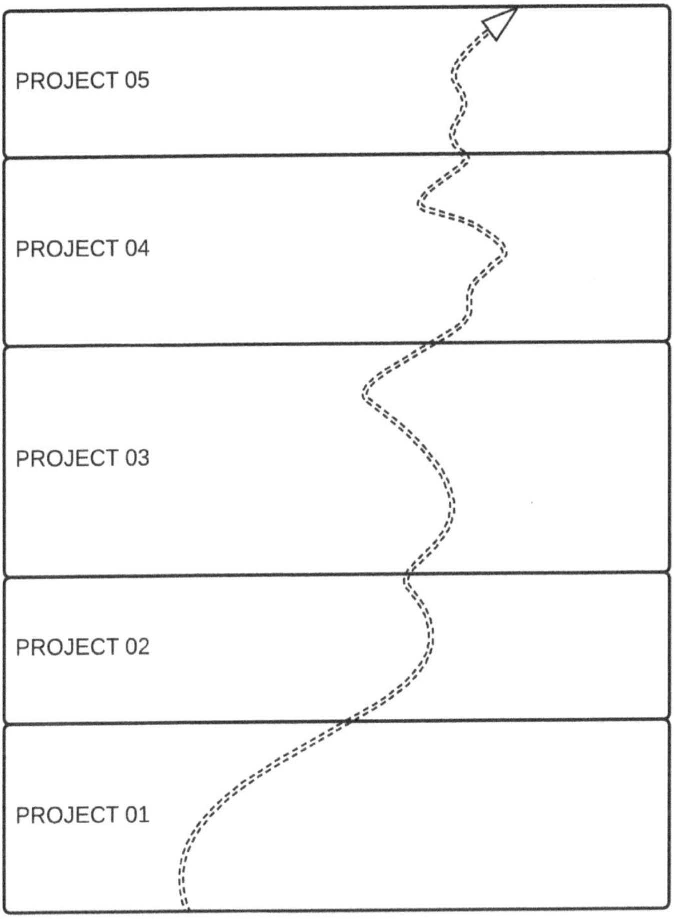

Figure 4.1 Imagine a line through multiple projects

language. It is a puzzle that requires you to contribute in order to feel the response of the game to the sound. You follow the path by creating it as you move forward. By the end, you'll have learned exactly how to make the game you just made, but no other game. Wayfaring is a continuous journey, and the wayfarer is always somewhere on the path.

Let's take a surfer's viewpoint. Like each approaching ocean wave, each game project is a unique variation, offering the audio director different possible lines through it – and exactly as though a surfer on a wave, the line taken is both followed and created simultaneously.

That line through multiple projects over the course of a career in sound for games may be thought about in the same way, as a line, just viewed from a wider vantage point.

If we visualize for a moment the line through the various aspects of a project, and subsequent projects we may see something like figure 4.1.

Knowing the general direction, we are flowing in, and having a north star to head towards is where vision and direction come into our wayfaring through projects. As we pass through each milestone, and subsequently each project, we respond to many small decisions, the problems that are right in front of us, day by day, hour by hour, and as we navigate towards the endpoint of the vision for each finished project, we eventually arrive in a unique place. To do this, we need to always keep the vision in mind; it may become clearer the nearer we get, or we may end up adjusting our vision of where we are going, but becoming distracted by the smaller things we encounter on the journey, things that may derail us from the overall promise, we need to be aware of those traps as directors. This is influenced by who we are, who is around us, what we are working towards. Only by taking this journey with our fellow developers, over time, can we eventually arrive at the finished game. The culmination of all the opportunities and trade-offs that we have negotiated, fought for and small paths we have either taken or not taken. We can't fully know the destination because we can't fully know the journey – until we take it – each journey is unique for each person.

In game audio development, this involves leading the whole process by focussing on the player experience. The end experience that the player will have on the sticks. If you begin with this, and sketch it, explore it, and always think about that, then the rest of the technology required, the features, the priorities, sounds, cues, and needs of the development will follow to support that onscreen vision of the experience.

The production and execution of that will also then be able to support that process through scheduling, benchmarking and understanding what inputs, outputs and dependencies are needed when. Production follows. Creative vision leads the needs of the technology, and production supports the execution of the vision.

An important element here is also that the experience of a wayfarer, perhaps through navigating multiple projects over the course of a career, teaches that every project is unknowable, even if it assumes an overall shape that is familiar. Going into a project, the knowledge and understanding that the path through it is not yet known reveals planning to be an act of faith (one that has flexibility built-in). We cannot know with precision anything that will happen on a project – and while we can have a fairly confident feel for what might be needed, it is not until the project unfolds that the shape of it is revealed behind us. These multiple traversals inform the experienced wayfarer with a set of survival mechanisms going into any new project, or any new role.

Key Elements of the Wayfaring Approach

Confidence

Being able to walk out into the unknown, taking the next steps knowing that the ground will be there to meet you. The secret here being that you create the ground beneath your feet by taking the step forward. The other secret being that you can get up and go again anytime you fall, or retrace your steps if you become lost, and it will seem, to an outside observer, like that was the intended path all along.

Flexibility

Any planning, any budgeting, any resourcing, and any direction and vision *must* be flexible to change and be built to respond to change from the ground up. You should treat it both as a deadly serious commitment, yet be capable of adjusting or completely changing it at the last second as new information and contexts develop. When you have finished a project, and look back, it may seem like this is the plan you had all along, but it is one that has been shaped by, responded and reacted through the process of discovery and responding to challenges. The line through the project is behind you and clear to see.

Vision

A wayfaring journey is a combination of exciting revelations, discoveries and challenges. Continually readjusting the overall details of the destination is a result. The vision of the end destination is not so much a fixed point that cannot be changed, rather an overall shape, impression or feeling that allows for details to manifest themselves as the team moves towards it. As the director of a team, you are looked to as a guide through this process. The journey through L1 first pass, to L2 identity, to the more confident and known L3 polishing pass is a good example of a wayfaring journey through an iterative process, building in layers, working quickly with purpose through each stage.

Craft Lines

In a similar sense to the overall line, we travel through our projects, every single interaction we have, every sound we make, conversation we have, integration we execute, each one of these actions can be thought of as a single 'brushstroke'. The interesting thing about a 'craft brushstroke' is that it is a composite blend made up of the three constituent colours of creative, collaborative and technical work.

I visualize and memorize this as a single golden line, rather than as three individually unmixed coloured lines; it is a way of elevating the brushstrokes to much more than just a composite of the three. Thinking about the craft of game audio as a combination of all three of those things is useful – you can't make a creative move without also needing to have a technical and collaborative move to support it – you can't make a collaborative move without bringing in creative ideas and technical manifestation, and you can't make a technical move without creative and collaborative aspects being taken into account. As a single act, blended together, at least in some measure of an ever-shifting balance that makes up the craft experience of our work. This is how I think about game audio as a craft, a blend of those three areas.

Eliminating Turbulence – Welcoming Friction

Getting the execution of an idea to feel like this single brushstroke is the part of the underlying overall goal of getting technology, tools, pipelines, and relationships to be frictionless – to the point that an idea or iteration can be followed through on the creative energy of its idea without hitting frustrations that stop that line of movement – instead, at each moment in the implementation, acquiring new knowledge about the problem and the solution, and making the necessary adjustments as the idea travels the pipeline and arrives onscreen in the engine. A surfer's board that is broken or damaged in some way, that lets the rider down at a key moment following the line, will be abandoned, burned in the next beach fire. At the same time, a board with a particular design, or flaw, that forces the rider to move in a certain way, on certain waves, can give rise to unexpectedly incredible moments and responses from the rider. This is why I now say 'turbulence free', rather than 'friction free' or 'frictionless'. Frictionlessness is as unattainable as true silence and mostly undesirable in collaborative ventures or wayfaring journeys. For me, turbulence-free describes the ideal environment we can achieve for working with our tools, teams and technologies in game audio; with the expectation and need for friction in the system, we have the ability to challenge ourselves and push further than we thought possible of ourselves.

Of course, this notion is about more than just tools and technology; it is also every bit about reducing any collaborative 'turbulence' that may be experienced with relationships on the team and in getting to know team members through working with them and their ideas, and in the same way, collaborative 'friction' being the thing that pushes us along and changes the way we think. The work on those relationships that needs to occur over time, through challenges, through compromise, through reaching understandings, is quintessential human game development craft. This is also interestingly a line along which we can travel as wayfarers. If I consider my relationship with my last creative director at the beginning, and then again at the end, it is an incredible journey filled with initial turbulence, friction, challenge, revelation, surprises and sometimes just awe and joy. Nothing is a fixed point.

The goal then is a 'turbulence-free' environment, where a flow of creative friction and challenge is welcomed, participated in, and enjoyed for the ways it pushes us further and challenges us as creative, technical and collaborative beings moving towards the promise of a vision.

5 Contexts

So, why can't an audio director also do hands-on work and get in the engine? They certainly can, to a degree, but it is further complicated by ever-changing context. There are several contexts we need to consider here, like technology, project scale and scope, creative team mindset, and the different production phases of each project that need to be understood to more substantially answer this pivotal question for an audio director.

Context 1: Historical Technology

Three Waves

The degree to which an audio director can actively get hands-on with content has changed a lot over time. To understand our current landscape towards 'direction' and away from being a hands-on Individual Contributor (IC), we can gain some clarity by thinking about where we are in terms of our current and past environment in games from both a craft and technology perspective.

I would define, generally speaking, three key waves of game audio technology that have shaped our craft over the past two and a half decades. Much like the craft evolution of coffee (an example from which I was inspired to think about audio technology in these waves), the following 'waves' represent distinct yet evolutionary phases of development.

- First Wave: Proprietary Technology. Up to and into the early 2000s, game developers relied on proprietary technology, creating and working with in-house game and audio engines. This era was characterized by unique, company-specific tools that offered no external access, necessitating individuals to join particular companies in order to work with and use these technologies.
- Second Wave: Middleware. The introduction and subsequent popularity of middleware marked the defining features of a second wave. Accessible third-party game engines like Unity and Unreal to some extent democratized development, while audio middleware such as FMOD and Wwise

DOI: 10.4324/9781003748465-6

offered more powerful tools for the sound designer, while encouraging less reliance on audio engineering support for every single small element of integration and implementation. This wave also introduced an environment where developers could learn and use these tools independently of working inside of a company, and could therefore acquire knowledge and develop expertise, *prior* to being hired at a particular studio that used the same tools.
- Third Wave: In our current wave, both proprietary and vanilla middleware tech stacks are complemented and augmented by bespoke proprietary software and scripting solutions that fulfil the needs of project-specific content pipelines, at the same time as relying on third-party middleware to form the base functionality. Modifiable audio environments like Reaper with custom scripts combined with middleware engines with more open APIs allow two-way communication, fostering custom innovation within existing frameworks.

Throughout these three waves, the audio director's role has evolved and shifted significantly. Within the first wave, the primary responsibility was getting sound to play, and in ensuring there was usable technology and tools for the playback of sound within very limited memory budgets, for example, ensuring music, dialogue, and sound were able to be pre-loaded or streamed. There was also a lot more freedom for the creation of the content itself in terms of processing, as very little, if any, Digital Signal Processing could be done at run time. The main concern was getting those sounds to play and be triggered in the engine at the right time.

Through the second wave, audio technology became less of a problem to overcome, but still had a significant gravitational pull on the work and of the director. DSP on the software side meant more emphasis on sound design at run time rather than being pre-baked – increased RAM also meant many more layers of sounds could be combined at run time. This gave rise to more iterative work and content creation moved into the audio tools, meaning greater emphasis on technical skills for sound design.

The third wave pushed design and implementation even further into the technical arena, meaning the director could spend even more time and attention on reviewing the top-level of sound that the player would experience. A split of creative audio directors and technical audio leads characterized this period, with one able to focus on the overall creative and cohesive vision of the sound, while the other focussed on the technology, toolsets and integration processes and teams that supported this vision.

A fourth wave may be said to be one of machine-learning-assisted pipelines where iteration on an always-running game build will be instantaneous for all disciplines. With this potentially comes a way of working that is challenging for disciplines that are dependent on upstream teams – like audio. This is a development environment in which anyone can change or tune anything at run time; meaning animations, lighting, level design are all fluid and mercurial. An art review may result in instant, live art changes. Audio, as the ultimate downstream dependency, will need somehow to adapt to this world of continual change through a variety of new approaches (regression checkers, auto-conform systems, and more production-savvy content locks and audio-only milestones).

Understanding where you are today, the technology and tools you can take advantage of, and how much automation vs hands-on bespoke functionality needs to be crafted is going to be a key factor in determining the shape of the role you need to play on any project. An audio director or leader on a smaller-scale project today, working in the third or fourth wave of audio technology, will be able to achieve a great deal more than those working in the first or second waves. However, there remain other contexts that also need to be taken into account.

Context 2: Project Scale

The scale of any project, and understanding it, is another essential area to figure out in terms of what work you might be doing as an audio director. A decision to go hands-on with some aspect of the sound is likely to be one you initially make in the spur of the moment. Then, after perhaps some time attempting to focus on this area, you may find you need to abandon that approach and delegate that area to another member of the sound team. Indie, Triple-I/Double-A or Triple-A/Quad-A all imply vastly different scales of project, with huge differences in team sizes and focus.

Audio Direction on a Small Team

The context of scale on a very small team may mean that, as a director, you are also able to work on and shape the sound design, dialogue design and integration, as well as music. Indeed, you may also be able to function as the music designer or composer on the project, as well as sound designer. Many of the decisions you make about integration will be informed by the content work you are creating. Having time and focus on this aspect is essential here, as with a small project, the implementation and production of the content may be relatively straightforward and not take up much time and focus.

Audio Direction on a Mid-Sized Team

The 'double-A'- or 'triple-I'-sized teams are similarly unencumbered by huge teams and departments, and can make decisions in a far more agile way, typically shipping games more quickly and for a fraction of the budgets of larger triple-A teams. An audio director may still have the focus or bandwidth to spend significant time on one or two areas of content creation, though most likely not all of it, and small multi-person audio teams are a common occurrence at these kinds of project scales.

Audio Direction on a Triple-A Team

Sometimes also known as quad-A development teams, these are very large teams, who also have multiple other development, or co-dev teams within the same development organization working on sections of the game. There is even further scope here for an audio director to focus on and direct the onscreen experience; co-ordinating, communicating and approving work from various teams at this huge scale. Huge development teams move forward through various milestones, often to very strict production deadlines each with specific goals.

Studio Direction

The context of scale continues with the notion of an audio director who is an overall Head of Audio, or Director of Audio, sometimes called Studio audio director, perhaps at a publisher level, or overall at an executive level, responsible for the various development teams helping to co-ordinate their audio approaches across different projects. This role requires focus on an overall strategic vision in which all the various studios and projects are considered from the highest level overall in terms of maintaining both high quality and operational efficiency at the business level. For example, the role of a very large publisher may be to organize and ensure creative, technical, and collaborative efficiencies (across multiple studios, through the sharing of technology, expertise, experience, and resources), are aligned. All of this demands an audio direction role that is at the same time visionary and practical, setting the overall roadmap for the next one, three and five years across all teams and projects at the studio, as well as communicating this, and any changes in overall strategy, outwards to all the various other team audio directors and leadership roles at those studios.

Context 3: Creative First: A Shift from Software to Entertainment

As an audio director moves into a role that considers the overall effect and impact of sound and its four food groups on the audience, this requires making an evolutionary leap into completely different areas of focus – the viewpoint will shift from thinking about the game development from a software development point of view, (what happens underneath the surface) to instead seeing what you are developing as *entertainment* – what happens on the *surface* that the player sees, feels, hears and interacts with.

This shift could be most often glimpsed when taking a game production outside of the usual four walls of the development studio, for example, if you take the game offsite to a post-production mix facility to complete a final mix pass in an isolated, focussed and calibrated sound studio environment. No longer being able to see the rest of the team working at their desks, or even to see the Devkit or Dev computer (they being relegated to a machine room) physically shifts your entire focus and attention to the screen, the controller.

A further element to this understanding, is that video game development is still fundamentally an iterative development practice and not a post-production practice. Post-production practices for sound design and audio direction are mostly how sound is taught – and rest on the idea that a sound designer, dialogue or music designer will be somehow working on the sound for a finished final piece of visual work whereby all that remains to be done is to apply final sync-sound to the visuals. This is never how video game sound development is practiced, even across more linear aspects such as cinematics.

Leading with the creative onscreen vision of the overall finished intent, rather than letting technology lead your decision-making, is another of the evolutionary steps that an audio director often has to take in order to pull themselves out of the constantly churning iterative environment. If an audio team is continually reacting to changes from upstream teams, then they will never be able to influence the overall direction. By having an audio director, whose job it is to get out of the iterative continuum, and to see ahead, working with the other directors, understanding the changes driving those upstream teams, and making decisions at the direction level, rather than *reacting* down at the iterative software or feature level, they can convey important information to the team in terms of priorities.

For me, this has come to be one of the defining features between an audio director and a sound designer or lead – distinguishing a clear boundary between hands-on work and direction work – if you are hands-on, you are by definition a part of the reactive continuum of iteration, on the back foot in terms of changes, always seeking approval for your work. With direction, you are *ahead* of the decision-making of even the upstream teams, deciding what is and isn't important to the project and the goals of the project or milestones at any one time. With hands-on work, in the iterative stream you need to be fully committed and in control to take those iterative responsibilities seriously. If you are out of the iterative stream, guiding the work, you have to take those responsibilities seriously. The crux of the question here is, to what extent can you successfully commit to either of these things at the same time? The age-old illusion of multitasking means that it feels like we can achieve more than one thing at the same time, though in reality we're only achieving a small distracted percentage of focus on each and losing a lot of momentum through continual task and focus switching. If we're distracted from driving the ship, we will miss big important things; if we're distracted from hands-on iterative work, we will miss details. This means we are not able to fulfil either of those roles to the level of excellence that they require. There are however, certain moments in a production when the needs of each may allow for this focus switching to take place… and where it may even be advantageous.

Context 4: Production Phases: Metamorphosis

While we have discussed the general impacts of scale, and of the increased team sizes and fragmented responsibilities of audio teams as technology has changed, the question of what an audio director needs to be, to each project remains dynamic – and it is not just the scale of the entire team or project that is essential to understand here, but the way that the scale and activities of the team change over the lifetime of the project itself – scaling from a small iterative team in the concept and pre-production phases, to a behemoth industrial production line towards the end. A director must similarly adapt their approach as these changes occur, or better yet, prepare and plan for those changes in advance.

What I tend to advocate for with most projects is a hybrid dynamic approach in which an audio director leads the smallest possible internal full-time team that they can through concept, pre-production, and early production, building it dynamically through two further phases and then downsizing at ship.

Keeping the core team small insulates the knowledge of the project's pillars and driving forces, and retaining that cultural expertise and familiarity within a small closely aligned group that can react and dynamically adjust their work methods and ideas without disrupting a larger team.

This team shape could be as simple and compact as an audio director (hands-on in terms of early content exploration and approvals, with the creative director's team – moving fast with them and sometimes ahead of them). An audio lead (who sets up the entire working project structure), pushes the audio build pipeline to be turbulence-free for the audio designers, as well as setting up the systems through which content will be played back and propagated in the game. This person may also be a senior technical sound designer who is able to work with the engineering team in lock step with their system work, so that audio follows much the same guiding principles laid out by the technical direction.

The early discovery phase doesn't need a huge team, and is served best by being extremely agile and open.

This notion of keeping things small in the most uncertain and iterative parts of the project plays to the strengths of a smaller team.

However, once the project gets through the various approval gates, and begins to ramp up into full production, the requirements of the team change considerably. A game in full production requires a sometimes massive amount of content to be produced, integrated, approved and polished – the team size and composition needs to scale up, sometimes dramatically. This move to a secondary phase leans into more discipline-focussed review work, more separation of responsibilities, and seeks to maximize the audio team's output of approved, validated work.

It is at this point that the needs of the audio director's role will transform into a pure direction role whereby they are continually reviewing and unblocking the work of a much larger team, working as closely with an L-level quality methodology as possible, so that production and the rest of the team have clear expectations of what is at first pass, what is supposed to carry the identity and feel of the project, and what is being pushed to final polish. So, we have a major shift from ideation and exploration, from discovery about the project, where some hands-on content work is advantageous for the director to understand the material – to team-wide execution. The execution phase is defined by a more structured approach, relying heavily on sharp production and communication.

The team itself, as alluded to earlier, will most likely scale up temporarily during this phase, most often in the form of flexibility allocatable co-dev resources joining the team in various roles and capacities. Hiring and building an internal team to support a temporary production phase isn't always possible if there are finite internal resources. In an increasingly laser-focussed time and resource-driven development environment, outsourced audio co-dev is one route that can relieve the risks associated with carrying a larger team into uncertainties of future projects and their early development phases. (There are, of course, exceptions to this, whereby there may be multiple audio resources across multiple dev teams within the same development studio whose projects are offset such that a full-time IC sound designer may jump into supporting the full production of the next project as it rolls around. However, these projects lining up is always a challenge, as well as having the sound designer feeling like they are permanently dropping into full production or shipping modes without appropriate rest and recovery). This secondary phase may also be characterized as a discipline-focussed production phase, focussed on pushing content through a pipeline.

A third and final metamorphosis must happen in which the entire team needs to get into shipping mode. This is where production and communication gears up even further with new red-lines about delivery of approved material becoming absolutely critical, and the co-ordination of all those upstream teams (such as level design and animation, and Visual Effects) all need to be coordinated with the downstream team of audio. This mindset treats prioritized tasks and bugs much more stringently when timing out deliveries, having the team only focussed on P1 priority tasks for example. The mindset of being able to complete everything that the team wants to must be abandoned here in favour of shipping a game that has the most important features and elements, and that the sound supports the most important needs of the game experience.

This is when polishing less important areas to the experience, like ambiences or reverbs is pushed to the back of the priority list, and the design of the most critical sound elements are pulled forwards. The most important areas are revealed during director reviews, and the list of P1 issues that come out of those reviews can vary dramatically – yes, sometimes a specific reverb or a background ambience moment can receive sudden attention and find itself the owner of a P1 must-fix polish task. The focus moves to supporting the overall experience, fully away from the more silo-leaning mentality of each discipline that defines the previous industrial production period.

It is then through the audio director and the audio team metamorphosing during these three periods, DISCOVERY, PRODUCTION, and Finalizing/ SHIPPING that we are able to operate at optimal levels throughout each period. The audio director needs to lead and co-ordinate this metamorphosis, and therefore needs to be capable of these changes.

One challenge I often see is an audio director coming out of the hard certainties of finalizing a project, and finding it incredibly difficult to adjust to the requirements of an audio director at the discovery phase of their next project – with all its softness, experimentation and uncertainty. In my experience, a lot of audio direction issues are around identity, and being able to explain the three phases and the three broad types of audio director needed at each of these three stages can help to clarify what is needed and what changes are coming next, allowing them to regain control.

An audio director in the early discovery phases of a project can be much more involved in the creation of content and on the actual set-up and experimentation of various aspects of the project from top to bottom, while remaining focussed on working with the director's group in finding the overall vision of the game. This is a period defined by openness, curiosity, learning, listening – lots of experimentation and time to make mistakes. Whatever the project wants to tell you, you are available to explore.

In the production phase, focus must turn to reviewing and approving work, so setting up these reviews and working closely with production teams to ensure that the pipelines and upstream deliverables are happening when they should be is a priority. Working with the team, reviewing their work onscreen, regardless of whether that is through work done by the internal team or whether it is done by external co-dev designers and integrators, no matter how the team is composed, the work must be reviewed and approved appropriately. This period can be characterized as a period of knowing your material as a director, being able to answer questions and offer meaningful feedback in reviews of the sound work provided by the team. While there is still some learning occurring here on the part of the director, as things come together onscreen, for the most part the direction should be clear to all, and expressed clearly at every opportunity. Production should similarly feel buttoned-up and in control. Ramping up the team and making sure everyone has a clearly defined role and expectation is a defining characteristic of this phase.

Lastly, a shift to finalizing or shipping requires a further metamorphosis of the director to being extremely strict about priorities and knowing what tasks will make the most impact in certain required areas. This period can be characterized by more strictness and less flexibility, and feels more decisive and in some instances, has a more aggressive and cold decision-making tone. This could be likened to a military operation in the field. In fact, you will often find these kinds of people in the industry called 'finishers' who go from project to project in that very role, getting games across the finish line (unsurprisingly, they often have military backgrounds). Audio directors will need to designate, approve and ensure P0 and P1 tasks and bugs are assigned and resolved; they will also need to pay attention to when and how team members roll off the project when their work ends.

It might be more helpful, and fun, to think of these different stages as different personalities that the audio director might inhabit, or as different aspects to our own personality that will move to the foreground at different times (Figures 5.1).

Discovery **The Dreamer**

Production **The Knowledge-Keeper**

Finalizing **The General**

So, the question of what kind of audio director you are isn't really one that can be answered in fixed terms, and while you may prefer one aspect of the role to others, the role must encompass all three of those personalities and types of working practice in order to effectively match the needs of a project going through its full life cycle. Because it is the changing nature and needs of the project that have these requirements of the director at their various

Figure 5.1 Audio director Metamorphoses throughout the project

Credit: Tom Jennings. tomjennings.me

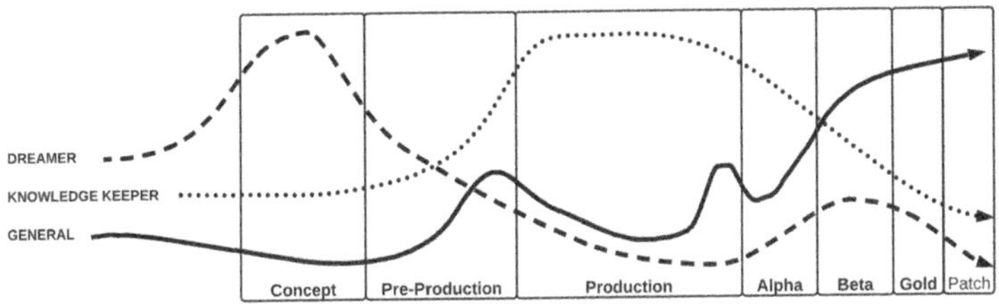

Figure 5.2 Illustration of three phases and their transitions

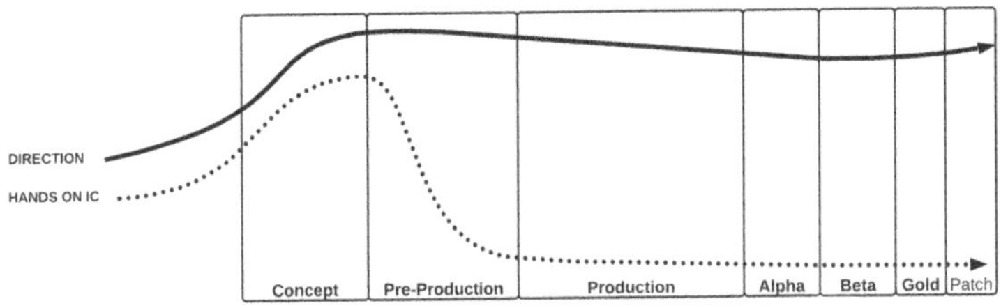

Figure 5.3 Life cycle of a project with 'Direction vs IC Curve'

phases, the director needs to respond accordingly with some pretty big chemical changes.

Though I have talked about these phases broadly, a director may also find themselves needing to be a general in one meeting, and a dreamer in the next, switching rapidly between archetypes based on the response required from each situation. There only being a predominant overall archetype when a particular phase or milestone needs to be met for a sustained period of time.

There is of course nuance in the transitions between these phases, as well as the necessity to carry some of each of these personality types during the other phases (yes, there can be a sudden shift to the finalizing mentality during the concept and pre-prod phase when the team is asked to produce a Vertical Slice, for example). But broadly speaking, these three stages of an audio director's life cycle throughout a project cover the changes that are necessary to support the team and the project (Figure 5.2).

That we get to occupy these three different personality types may suit some people more than others, and many of the problems arising in audio direction for games tend to deal with the transitions between these three distinctly different personality types, as well as the problems associated with hiring one particular personality type who can be massively unsuited to the other two. If we hire the finalizing style military general and expect them to get a project and a team through the carefree experimental phase, we may run into some turbulence here as they adjust, or try to shape the concept phase into a set of militarily achievable deliverables.

Similarly, a carefree experimental hire, brought on to ideate and be creatively free on a project, will encounter major challenges if they cannot then move into the buttoned-up production phases of the general-style role of finalizing.

Listening to the project and its needs is crucial to understanding metamorphism, as some less experienced teams will not be able to recognize when a certain boundary transition is happening, or is needed. This can also be an opportunity for audio directors to lead in communication clarity for the rest of the team, by identifying these rhythms of the project. An experienced audio director has likely had experience of all three of these roles to varying degrees and can spot when it is appropriate to 'change gear' and conjure the necessary personality for each stage.

As always, communication and presence are essential here; signalling and describing the changes that are going to occur at each stage to the rest of your teams (both audio and general), is important in order to that they are not left reeling from sudden crash shifts in approach. Being able to map out and to some extent 'feather' between those transitions is increasingly important in *managing* all of this.

Another of the challenges with audio direction is that all three of these personality types can eventually feel as though they are mushed together into a single blurry mess. Every day, each of these personality types can feel like it is being called upon to varying degrees. Integrating these into a single, agile identity that can be a dreamer in one sentence, and a General in the following sentence, is a step towards mastering the role of the director, and always done where appropriate with the right intensity at the right time, sensing where those shifts may be needed. Even using terms like 'ok, I am going to switch gears now' to indicate controlled changes, is a useful cue that communicates that it is not your personality or mood that is influencing a change in tone, but the necessary change to address the situation.

Also having different production vocabularies is very common here in these switches. Using terms like 'we need to have a conversation about that' denotes more serious intent, while a 'let's just try it out and see what happens' shows more adaptable openness to the outcomes. They each have their appropriate contexts and can play an important role in switching the tone and context of the team. So, just as an audio director needs to change lanes between these approaches, so the team also must follow. As sound designers, dialogue designers, and the various specialists and other roles in game audio development, it is important for you also to understand the particular moment that a project is in, and to understand the tone, and the vocabulary being used to denote the seriousness vs playfulness that you may need to respond with.

As we discuss changes in intensity and ways of expressing intention in a collaborative team context, there is however, a zero tolerance that should be in place for anger. It has no place or role in any of these personalities or ways of expressing a vision to the team, it always shows that you are not in control. Anger is a human emotion and will need to be outlet somewhere, but not in front of the team. You are always modelling behaviour to your team, and they will always be feeling and watching what happens closely. With any anger-based reaction, you will always have to back-pedal and apologize, which while perhaps humanizing you, will also undermine the way the team sees you and relies on you for direction. Anger manifests a fear-driven environment, and having team members who will not give you information or express concerns out of fear you will react angrily, means that problems will build and remain unseen, unresolved, unexpressed, and invisible to you. Recognize that anger is present, go away, calm down, and come back clear-headed. Anger always passes, so it has no value or contribution to your decision-making or relationship building on the team. Dealing with colleagues when they are angry is itself a skill and a challenge, making sure to call them out in front of others and asking them to come back and continue when they are calm – having other people around when you do this is extremely important.

The audio director then, must be a dynamic being, who can calibrate themselves and their thinking to the needs of a project at a particular period of its production, and then metamorphosize themselves to suit the demands of each subsequent phase – all around a central identity as a director and vision holder for audio.

To illustrate this more simply in terms of our original question about hands-on and hands-off work, and when each is appropriate, we can visualize a curve to show where an audio director might have the opportunity and possibility to jump in on hands-on work, and also where they will need to pull back and focus on direction. As with previous production curves, this is simply to show that our role and activities are dynamic, and have finite life-cycles within a project before they need to shift (Figure 5.3).

6 Healing

Starting (Again) with a Blank Page

Due to the combination of very high expectations and generally broad and undefined responsibilities, many audio directors become overwhelmed. How they got there is often an accumulation of many compromises. Overwhelmed with accountability, responsibility, emergent tasks, pressure, and stress (both externally from other parts of the team and internally from pressure put on themselves). Some may believe this to be a normal state of being, and that this continual feeling of stress and pressure, as well as the constant sense of needing to work on something, goes with the territory and perhaps the (slightly) higher pay cheque. However, this state of stress should not be normalized, nor is it sustainable, and rarely does it lead to good work or team outcomes. Anyone going through overwhelm, who is constantly being pulled in multiple directions by requests from every corner of the team, will feel their decision-making to be muddied, their priorities simply dictated by who is the loudest person in front of them asking for something, and their rest time is insufficient for them to fully recover and see things more clearly.

The Two-Day Reset

Whether you are starting out on a new project for the first time, or already deep into a project as a veteran, what can help bring clarity to these overwhelming situations is a complete reset. This is time that is carved out specifically to focus on stripping everything back to the most fundamental building blocks, and figuring out what the responsibilities of the audio director and the team members need to be, as well as how to move forwards with a more balanced approach. The reset exercise I will describe here takes two days, but you can certainly take any time you need to get through this process.

This reset process can also become an important ritual at several key moments on a project, for example as a team moves from pre-production into production, or from production into finalizing.

DOI: 10.4324/9781003748465-7

Before You Start: Create Space for Focus

To see things clearly, we need a distraction-free space. If we are reacting to a new crisis every hour, every minute of the working day, we can never hope to reach a place where we can see things clearly. The time and focus space taken to do a reset must be protected at all costs, someone knocking on the door or popping up on a Slack message to ask for something urgent is always going to derail the whole thing. So, ensure you have completely blocked off your time for these two days and are unavailable with phones off and screens off – and ideally you have left the game development space entirely, to go through this process and that people on the team know you are unavailable for a while.

You may do this alone (certainly doable, but not recommended), or you may include a trusted team member, but try to keep it very limited. I would recommend a trusted producer to go through this with.

To create time and space for this, I recommend delegating everything to your team while you are away. It shows trust, and they will rise to any challenges in your absence.

Important: Delegating your team to fight all the immediate fires allows you to do the fire prevention work needed that lies ahead. Assign a main point of contact, and set out-of-office replies. There is likely to never be a 'good time' to do this, so jump in and get the most out of this time. To be able to reconnect with and renew the grasp on the vision and subsequently line up the technical roadmaps and production schedules that support it is the goal here.

7 Day One

Seeing It All

Once you have carved out some protected thinking space, the first step of the process is to simplify. If you wish to do some pre-reading before you go into this, I highly recommend reading both John Maeda's *The Laws of Simplicity* and Greg McKeown's *Essentialism*. These outline very well the kind of overall transformations that you will need to go through to more fully achieve these steps.

Simplification can also be thought of as a process of reduction. Reduction is an approach that needs to be at the heart of an audio director's worldview. Keeping it simple. Complexity is always going to be present, but can spiral and be paralysing when viewed flat. A focus on fewer things, at higher priorities, gives back control.

Taking time to sound out the entire jumble of responsibilities, begins by simply throwing all of those areas against a wall so you can take a step back and look at it all. This is about making everything visible. This could be post-it notes, or on a whiteboard, any method whereby you can see everything in its big, messy, unorganized, overwhelming totality. You may start with current high priorities, adding other areas less urgent, as you exhaust the list, give it time and keep adding things no matter how trivial they may appear. Visualize everything, no matter how big or small.

Once you have thrown all the areas at the wall, the first step of the reduction process can begin… categorization or grouping.

I recommend a circular view as it allows you the most space and also creates an important gravity centre for decision-making and approvals. You can put a single post-it at the centre… 'Vision' (Figure 7.1).

Categorize

Now you have everything up there in front of you, you can start to sort into common categories. You may also find yourself creating subcategories, and also any larger container categories that may occur to you. The goal here is to organize the mess of things, into self-contained *broad* subject areas. From an audio design lens, it can be a little bit like organizing a messy multi-track

DOI: 10.4324/9781003748465-8

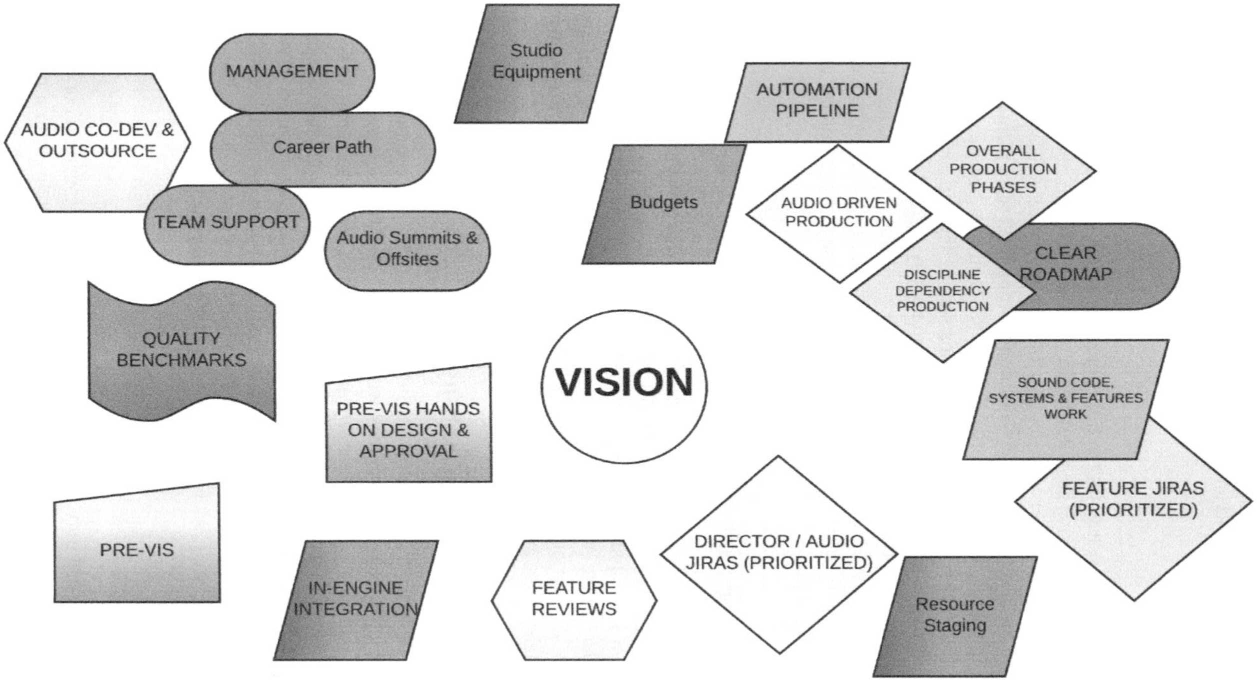

Figure 7.1 Everything on the board circular diagram, Vision at the centre

session into folder and group tracks and sub-tracks or containers, grouping as you go until it is all organized.

The Team

It is normal, as you go through this process, to get a terrifying sense of the overall scope of work areas for audio, and that you will also start to think about the team members or resources that you may have.

You can also make post-it notes representing each team member. For the team members, whether internal or external, you may also start to have an organizational pass on the board, perhaps placing them in a reporting hierarchy or by seniority. Perhaps it is the hierarchy they currently have, or perhaps it is a new one that you might need to move towards, keep them as flexible players on the board, move them around, see how things look. You may also then start to assign a team member to have ownership over particular categories as you organize.

The Project

With the team and the various areas of responsibility up on the wall, you have all the separate components, but the project and its needs are going to shape the team and requirements you really need. Write up somewhere on the board the pillars of the project – these are usually supplied and evangelized by the creative director or game director. It is important to have these written down, influencing the way you organize all the elements on the board.

Accountability vs Responsibility

If you do have a larger team structure that incorporates a combination of its production capabilities, perhaps with external co-dev resources, it is very important to assign *accountability areas* (ability to review and approve work, the keepers of the quality bar) to internal team members, and any *responsibility areas* (delivering the work itself) to any external team members. Having some colour-coded post-its differentiating internal team members as well as external resources can be useful here as a part of that process. Remember, you can outsource the work but not the accountability for the quality of that work.

Inheritance

Another area that may come out of this process is the recognition or realization that you have perhaps inherited a structural hierarchy from a previous audio director, or from a way that the company and team have been built. Perhaps the team has been making a certain kind of game which is why the team is currently structured the way it is, but now needs to make something different. It is important to remove all of those inherited structures and think clearly about what the current needs of today's team and today's project are.

Moving Things Around

As you start to build up your new picture of structure, moving around containers and grouping areas, the complexity of the work at hand has not been changed fundamentally, but the way it is organized and assigned to owners, folds all that complexity into a framework that should feel more simple and compact.

As a director, carrying unorganized complexity in your head can be a huge burden, and using organizational principles to subcategorize and hide that complexity in container subject areas is a necessary survival strategy. Assigning those areas to owners further reduces your exposure to overreach. As a director, you still have accountability for everything on the board, but only at the top levels that you can more comfortably review and approve.

As alluded to, team size and project scale play huge roles in determining what the audio team needs to look like. You may also identify gaps as you go through this process, additional resources that you may need but do not have. Technologies can play a role here too, if there is time, perhaps technology features can be put in place on the board that enables designers and supervisors to cover more work across more areas without losing focus, subsequently some reduction in the necessary team bandwidth may flow out of this.

It is important not to overburden team members with multiple broad areas of responsibility, the more task switching a single person has to do, the less effective they become at owning each area. One of the goals here is also to create *focus and ownership* on one or two specific, ideally related, areas for team members and resources.

Not only can the rest of the development team now know who to go to for collaboration on those specific areas, but the audio team members themselves understand much more on far deeper levels about each area, and invest far more care and attention into them through ownership. By having autonomy over how problems are solved and approached in each major area, that person is able to fully invest and know clearly what they are responsible for. This may sometimes be referred to as Pillar Ownership, meaning a subcategory, or sub-pillar area of the audio production (for example, weapons, environmental ambiences, or abilities) is owned by one specific point of contact. This could also be done more vertically by assigning map (or level) ownership, having a lead or sound designer assigned to have complete ownership over the delivery of specific maps. This all depends on the type of game and how the rest of the team works on those aspects of the game – sometimes this ownership structure is expressed as strike teams or feature teams – small teams who collaborate together with co-ownership responsibility over a map or feature. Try to reflect this in your grouping (Figure 7.2).

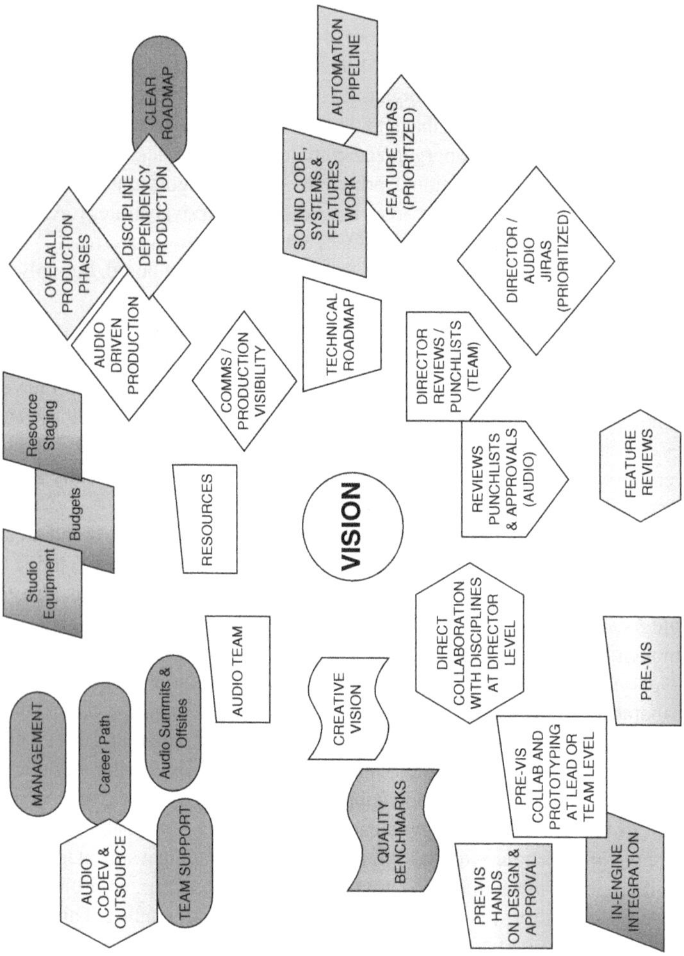

Figure 7.2 Organized diagram

Reduction: Shrinking the Field of Responsibilities

As for the audio director, your accountability lies with those broadest top-level groups, or containers, so the creative vision at the centre, then the technical roadmap, all the reviews and approvals, production visibility and communications, running the team through continual conversations and unblocking them with any issues they bring to the surface which they cannot themselves solve, or where they need more clarity of direction.

So, we're going to add an inner circle and an outer circle to the diagram to illustrate those areas within the audio director's accountability zone, and the rest of the team's responsibilities zone… (Figure 7.3).

You'll see the closest gateway areas are still within the audio director's inner circle; however, you can even hand over ownership of some of these gateway areas to a lead, provided you continue to retain overall *accountability* and approval sign-off on the general plans and approaches, so you may step back even further to sitting atop of those areas and co-ordinating them, helping and guiding them by using the vision.

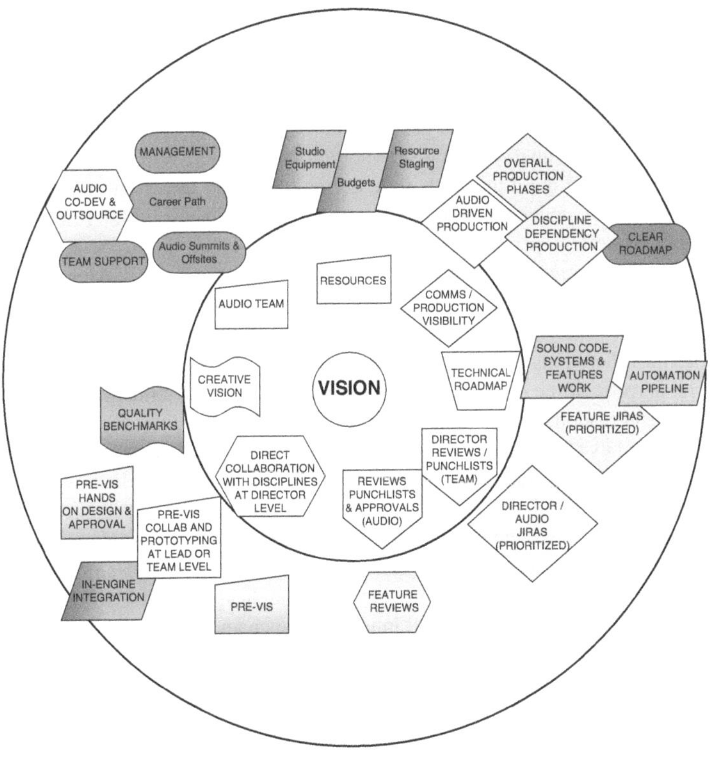

Figure 7.3 Reduced field of responsibilities around inner circle

Your role at the centre of the diagram is to continually prioritize and understand the most important things. Understanding the entire context and experience of the game onscreen.

Having your attention close to the centre of this circle also allows you to have a more objective view of what is important and also what is of lower priority – it means you are able to stay connected to the other directors (who are also working at this same level) and the day-to-day changes on the direction of the project that have critical meaning for the priority of those areas outside the circle and out at the furthest edges.

Sure enough, this approach of responsibility at the centre of the circle mirrors closely the job descriptions and established definitions and working practices of Art Directors – who typically come into a project with the sole aim of directing the art team and working with them to achieve and adapt where necessary, the overall vision and how everything fits into context.

Timelines and Roadmaps

As a next step on day one, we should now consider the element of time. For this we need the technical (or feature) roadmap and the production (road to ship) timeline, as these are two other important areas belonging to the project.

The technology and production plans will be an expression of the project goals, and it is important to ask questions that answer clear priorities… is time, money, or quality the most important thing? There will inevitably be a combination of these things that are deemed critically important to any project, however, understanding the most important will be useful for you from a planning strategy perspective.

For this exercise, all that is really needed are the main dates. Alpha, Beta, Gold Master, Day 0 patch, Day 1 patch. Put these up on a separate area next to your circle. Where you are today, and how much time you have remaining will exert another major influence on how you organize all the areas and resources. The purpose of the project roadmap's presence is to exert influence over your team and responsibility structure. When you realize and truly see how much time you have left, it sharpens your ability to cut, group, delegate, and reduce.

Roadmaps are highly collaborative elements that need to be worked on in conjunction with the technology teams and production teams respectively. But simply taking them into consideration here, rather than changing them, as part of your organization and planning can bring an important dimension to your process – highlighting remaining time and the question of 'when?'

It is most likely that you will inherit both tech and production plans from those respective teams, rather than being present at their inception (although this is possible and an excellent opportunity to begin thinking about sound dependencies and having that influence the planning of the project). It is important to build and map your organizational plans or changes 'into' those inherited timelines, and also to flag areas where there is either too much time (or too little) currently assigned. These are collaborative conversations and negotiations you will be able to have later with production. Another reason why having a trusted producer go through this process with you is useful.

Production plans will also continue to inform you of the key values of the project. Time may not be an issue for example if you are on a project with a small team who has no publisher deadlines and is there to make a passion project however long it takes. Having a strict budget will also give you very clear redlines where work can and cannot be done, a budget constraint enables you to prioritize features, and strip away any nice-to-have elements of the game in favour of the most critical elements. A quality redline can similarly allow you to scale the work on the project and the team shape and size to meet that need. This process of understanding what kind of approach will resonate strongly with the rest of production will help you to make the right decisions in your audio planning.

It is at this stage, as you dive into the production and technology roadmaps, that our initial diagram starts to feel the need for some additional layering of organization. We start to run into organizational principles driven by the project needs. For example, a lower budget may force you to deprioritize or cut feature areas, focus on fast iteration using more simplified implementation techniques. Perhaps focusing on off-the-shelf solutions rather than investing time in building custom features from the ground up – though these still take time to implement – is a better path forward. Prioritization forces you to (re) evaluate your production planning and technology and tools efforts in efficient ways, and in terms of efficiencies, we are looking to resonate with and amplify the project's financial, time, and quality goals.

End of Day One

So, reconnecting with these realities of large projects, and their needs from an audio director, is an important part of any reset/recalibration process. By mapping everything out and then simplifying and reducing, we see the importance of moving away from hands-on responsibility, but also the importance of retaining overall review and approval of those areas.

So, on day one, we've extracted and reduced all the day-to-day responsibilities and looked at the team through the lenses of the project vision and the timeline. On day two, we are going to go further still into what the audio director is ultimately responsible for, but at a much higher level.

Importantly, this needs to happen after good sleep.

8 Day Two

Defining the Vision

Problems and stresses tend to resolve and compress overnight into dew drops of clarity – diamonds of the morning. Write them down before they're gone, and bring them to day two.

Looking again at your reorganization should feel good; anything that was perhaps still unresolved may feel easier to resolve now with a fresh perspective, so feel free to continue the organizational tweaking until it feels right.

As we fully get into day two, we are going to shift focus now on the core responsibilities of the Audio Director, as it is actually these things that you spent the day yesterday freeing yourself up to focus on.

Even with just oversight across all the categories that were broken out on day one, we're talking about a lot of areas that can still feel overwhelming… Is there perhaps a way to have just one element that we can focus on as directors? Direction, fundamentally at the highest level, is about one thing… vision.

This could be described as developing a creative vision of a game being made, validating and communicating that vision, and then helping the various people on your team, and across other teams, to get there through their work onscreen. It could also be expressed as a vision you have for the team making that game, their relationship with technology and automation, a particular size or shape, with particular people or owners on that team. It could also be a vision for a certain kind of development studio or environment, remote, physical, hybrid, where particular practices, attitudes, and values are important.

Across these different areas, the vision is something that you know; you can see it and sense it; it is pulling you towards it, but it is not reality yet. It may be very far from the reality you find yourself in every day. Seeing it and feeling it, having a sense that it is possible is the initial impulse of a vision. Expressing it is the next step, followed by putting the world in motion to move towards it.

In game audio development, and in audio direction specifically, we need exactly that, a vision for these three overall areas, and it is articulating these groups that we are going to tackle with our Day 2 focus.

We can begin with the project. You'll need to have a vision for a project, the creative audio pillars that resonate for the game, but specifically for audio.

DOI: 10.4324/9781003748465-9

Write down your initial vision statements under the heading 'Vision: Project' (we will tweak them later, don't worry, the important thing at this stage is to get something written down immediately).

The project then demands that a vision is provided for the team needed to make that project, this could be anything from a small core team of generalists who are passionate experts in the type of game being made, or it could be a large co-ordinated team growing and shrinking through different phases, bringing in specialists where needed etc. Write these team pillars down under the heading 'Vision: Team'.

This team then in turn needs an environment in which they will work on the project. These are values and ways of working that you may see as fundamental to supporting the team working sustainably over time and under certain pressures. Write these pillars, or values, or ideas down under the heading 'Vision: Environment'.

Three Vision Elements: Interconnected

Next, we are going to connect these three areas. Inspiration for how to visualize this connection of vision areas and their relationship came to me from skimming the pages of *The Surfer's Journal*, and seeing an advertisement for the outdoor clothing company Finisterre. They happen to have a fascinating logo down in the corner of some of their print advertising that always caught my eye. It is a circle, inside of which is a flowing triangle, of three areas, graphically connected; labelled with text: *product, environment, people.* After a bit of further investigation, the shape appears to be based on, or at least includes in its design, a *triquetra* or Celtic knot, which is used traditionally to represent unity and interconnectedness. I like this visual a lot, it is very memorable, no matter how stressful and turbulent a project may become, this isn't the sort of thing that can be dislodged from the mind (Figure 8.1).

Porting this over into context for our audio vision areas… 'Product' can be re-interpreted as the 'Project', the game, or experience that is being made. 'People' can be translated over to 'Team', the people making the game; the audio team specifically. 'Environment', here I interpret as including two factors; the ecosystem of tools and pipelines, as well as the culture of the studio, the support networks and values in place that nourish and support the team (Figure 8.2).

This is an exciting representation of interconnected vision because this shows a system of three categories that are feeding one another, each flowing into and out of the others. This rings true, as a decision made in any one of those areas will have impacts in the others. These three elements are about the best overall categories we can have for delineating the different areas of sound work on a game development team. Again, it is simple, memorable, and makes the entire vision easy to communicate to the team, or to refer back to in meetings and challenging moments when you need to make decisions.

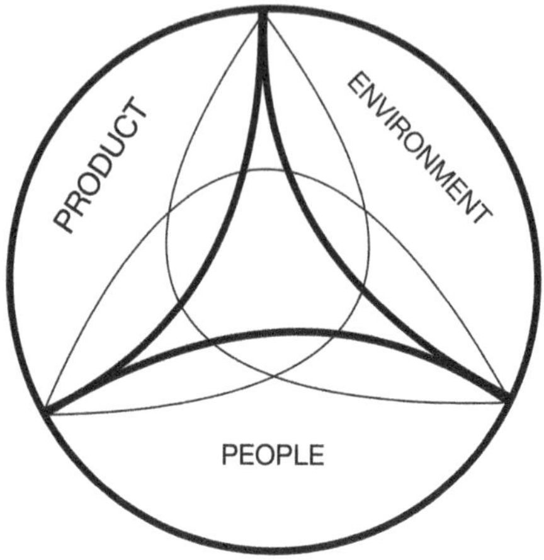

Figure 8.1 Finisterre logo

So, this gives you, as an audio director, a central vision to work from. All of these elements need attention and care every day, you'll be reinforcing these things in almost every decision and communication. It is how we relate to the project, the team and the environment in which the game is being made – it is how we maintain any drift away from these fundamental statements. It stops us also from having moods or personal tastes too heavily influencing what we communicate to the team in terms of direction. It ensures we have a platform that we can offer consistent direction *from*. As a director, it is essential that you are consistent in the way you evaluate the work of the team onscreen. If you give notes based on your mood that day, or your ever-shifting personal tastes, or the sound of the latest thing you just played, these are somewhat random elements that can be wildly inconsistent from day to day. Once you have a consistent set of lenses through which to provide notes and feedback, you can remain consistent.

How we manage these areas is continual work, and again, we have to work here with a mindset that a single action has impact across all three of these areas. A decision made as director to solve a problem on the project will likely have impact on the people and place require support from the environment. In similar ways, any decisions involving people will elicit responses in the spider web from other areas of this ecosystem.

Using the rest of day two, transfer the areas of vision you have previously written down under each heading of Project, Team and Environment into a Triquetra and looking again at them should allow you to tweak and adjust what is there. Look out for any areas where there is repetition, and see where you can reduce that. By the end of day two you should have a nicely compact, boiled-down, memorable vision.

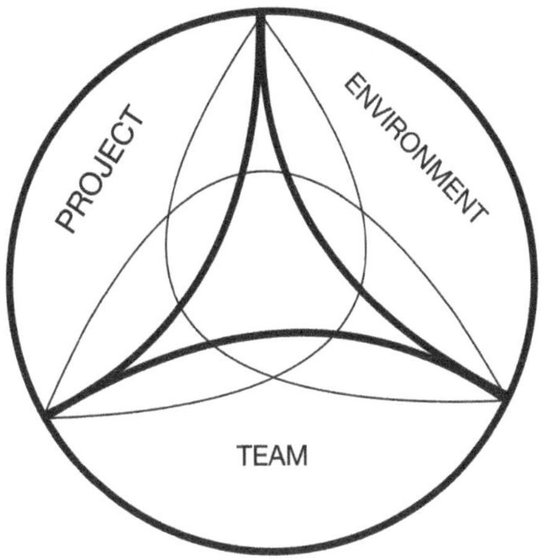

Figure 8.2 Example audio vision triquetra

Any time you are asked to provide or explain your vision, you can respond by drawing or showing the triquetra, learning to quickly draw one on a whiteboard is also a new skill you can acquire here, and most people will not be expecting such a fully rounded vision (Figure 8.2).

This second day of focus, then, forces you to set out the key elements of what will drive your work as a director, now you are freed up to focus on direction. It also provides a framework for how the work of the team can be both evaluated and supported. By having a vision that is interconnected in this way, you are able to understand, manage, and express the entire vision, rather than just addressing a single dimension of it.

With the two-day reset process now complete, you can now begin the work of communicating the changes you have made back to your leadership team and then out to the rest of your team, putting in place any new responsibilities and transition plans in collaboration with the rest of the production and leadership teams.

As mentioned, it is not uncommon to have to go through this process a few times over the course of a large project, especially if the overall scope or requirements change significantly, but also as you and the team readjust to the very different realities of prototyping, full production, and finalizing a game.

9 Vision Work

Practicalities, Processes and Techniques

The previous chapter assumed you have some notion of the vision already defined and are easily able to write it down and express it in simple pillars or bullet points. But what are some processes for distilling ideas down into these pillars?

The stages and working process of creative visionary work, whether for a feature, or an overall level, map or character, or even for a team or a development environment, can be simplified thus: from the dream to the page to the screen.

First, Imagine It

The inner dream/feeling and promise of the thing you can see/hear/feel – spending time tending to this inner vision feels like it could be 'just' day-dreaming, but it is crucial time that is needed in getting to know what the inner vision is.

Second, Express It

Capture it, sketch it, prototype it, show it, and collaborate with key partners on refining the shape of the idea. This can and should happen quickly. How do you get people to come along with you? Capture the vision visually, and talk through it – honing on paper so that its shape is clearer and becomes communicable. Take notes and get feedback, but stay true to the initial idea. Start to find key words that elicit the right tone for your ideas.

Lastly, Do It

Take real action to move towards it. Take a first step along the path. This could be a more detailed prototype or pre-visualization step for approval. Remove anything that moves away from your vision feeling, and add things that pull

DOI: 10.4324/9781003748465-10

you closer towards it – exploring dead-ends that may feel right, or could be interesting areas, but in the end don't resonate is also crucial; knowing those paths are *not* a part of the vision are just as important as moving towards it.

Visions, on their own, aren't really anything but a fleeting daydream. They can be a mood, a certain sound, the way the light in a certain place or a line of dialogue suggests an entire world. Capturing it in some way, expressing it, writing it down, is a way for you to have quick access to it again. Then, via further exploring where it leads you through pre-vis sketching, this is the part that brings it out of the subconscious and to the surface, landing it on the shore. From there, it becomes a process of action and practical work to get it onscreen and playable – all the time checking back and adjusting against the initial feeling of the original vision – at this stage, you are now actively in the process of direction. Vision leads to direction, and direction is nourished by vision.

Now, while vision holding may sound easy and simple, it is very occupying, and you may spend a long time fixated on the inner vision. This is also the work of a director, to be a vision holder; staying true to the inner vision while putting its creation into action through practical and achievable terms and forms.

Though it can be achieved at various stages and scales of game development, the work of direction does not require any deep, detailed craft-level execution or implementation by the director themselves. It does not require sound design, music composition, or hands-on mixing. The craftspeople on your team are looking to you to be the force that animates *them and their work* towards the idea – allowing them to go too far, to find the edges, to discover what locks in and feels right.

So far, I have spent a lot of time telling you that there is little to no hands-on work to do as a director and a vision holder. Yet, there is a category of hands-on work that belongs to and enables an audio director to explore and express a vision more clearly – we might more generally call this 'vision work', and there are several categories here that can fall under the nomenclature of pre-visualization, sketches, or proof of concept. The difference here is this hands-on exploratory work is driven by speed – sound design, music or dialogue sketches and mixes, made quickly using any kind of pre-existing or even bespoke material as a way to quickly validate an idea, to be able to check it against your original feeling as you build it up in layers, and being able to then show the creative director and the other directors on the team in order to give them a sense of the feeling you have for the sound. Playing these quick audio sketches, rather than explaining your vision, is the only way to properly communicate and further validate any audio idea.

10 Early Stages

Discovery Phase

As an audio director, in the beginning, it is my responsibility to listen. Not to talk too much, but to get excited about what I am hearing. Listen to the project, the game design being articulated, the people making it, what is exciting them, the other voices, understand and explore what it is, where it wants to go, what it wants to be, and what it could be. You will also get a sense here of what is known and what is unknown, showing you some opportunities for fast audio exploration and validation. Your gift to a team at the early stages is to be capable of using sound, music, and voice, exploring what the mostly imagined experience could sound like and feel like. When it is time to speak, our role is most often to give voice to that which has no voice – the things about the experience that cannot be seen, but that can only be felt, which in the end, provides a deeper understanding of the new game experience being created. Being able to articulate this experience and how it feels, when it becomes possible to do so, is one of your biggest responsibilities to the project.

An additional side effect of listening, and in taking time to consider before speaking, to respond rather than reacting, is that it gives your voice a sense of reliability and trustworthiness. It could be said that the power of those that always speak diminishes the more they speak. Yours is the voice whose power silently grows.

With regards to establishing any vision and its direction, we may use a simplified graphic pencil-illustration analogy – begin with the gestural – get the overall impression of the game sound world down – then when this is resonating, feeling exciting, move to the structural, filling in some basic detail, resolving specific areas and features, all the time working within the parameters of the established gestural direction. For gestural we might use a certain pencil or stroke style, and then move to a different pencil or stroke style for structural marks. Finally filling in detail with another pencil type and stroke style. This very closely matches the L-level approach of 'building' up the sound work in layers, continuously iterating and refining each stage at certain fidelity levels, allowing for increased velocity and focus at each stage.

DOI: 10.4324/9781003748465-11

Moving away from technical audio jargon in multi-discipline contexts is critical in being able to communicate and associate more effectively across disciplines. Speaking and working in evocative, emotional, or structural language, ensures that everyone remains on the same page when it comes to the overall *effect* that the game or feature might have for the audience.

Learning the Internal Vernacular of the Project

Working alongside the creative team, you will start to drink in their influences and become more familiar with their shared reference points, while also bringing in some of your own references that resonate well with the project. This internal vernacular, or local language, of the project, will express itself as a series of references that can come from anywhere, but often from other forms of expression, movies being one of the most commonly used due to it also being an audio-visual medium. But I have been on projects where poems, pieces of music, places and locations, and buildings are all used to evoke a certain feeling or tone of a game being created. All of these elements will collectively form a commonly spoken and understood vernacular for the team and the evocation of the creative and practical vision of the game. The more time you spend on the project, among the team and their influences, the more you will naturally learn and find yourself speaking in the project vernacular.

Pre-Vis

Any hands-on work, such as the pre-vis listed above, in which the audio director may spend some time working on concepts within a Digital Audio Workstation or simple integration examples, fall into the pre-visualization, or pre-vis, category. This work is often necessary in order to have the vision more deeply understood by the audio director, providing some initial validation of the materiality of the sound world and to understand it from a hands-on viewpoint. This aspect of getting to know a project through materiality benefits the audio director by having them understand what works and what doesn't from the inside out.

By knowing if an approach requires specific kinds of layering or processing, whether there is a minimal or maximal density in the design, if it requires synthesis or recordings of authentic sound - all of these elements become strong building blocks and direction tools later on when the audio director becomes more necessarily hands-off in the process.

In referring back to these initial pre-vis design sessions and their creation process, a director can certainly better lead the team to create work that is of a similar feel. Of course, the other primary purpose of hands-on pre-vis is to collaborate with and receive approval from, the game director or creative director, as well as resonance and feedback from the rest of the discipline directors.

This process of sharing the work in progress, getting as many feedback notes as possible throughout the process, and presenting the material more broadly to the team for even further feedback is an important aspect of being visible with your direction work. If at any point the work does not resonate, it is essential to quickly get those notes and be able to think about and adjust the tone or structure of the sound.

Any feedback in the initial phases is extremely valuable to the pre-vis process, navigating the design and, above all the feeling that the sound will bring to the experience. This is best done often and early when adjustments and experiments are cheap and easy. All work is to be considered throwaway in this process, as it is the process itself that is the most important aspect of the work here, getting to know the project and the rest of the team, and running up against as many of the core ideas that support that overall experience as early as possible – this is the primary objective. When this time period ends, and the team heads into a more production-centric rhythm, the goal is, ideally, that the knowledge about what works and what doesn't is available to the director and expressible through pillars, rather than a sense that this is still work that needs to be widely explored.

Early Interactive Prototyping

Some elements of in-engine integration will likely form some part of the pre-vis efforts, at least some proof-of-concept or ways of getting an initial feel for an interactive element or feature itself. This can be to get the feel of the explorations in the game and onscreen early, working alongside the interactive feature developments of the rest of the team. This kind of exploration in-engine will slow down the speed at which you may be able to try out quick ideas in the DAW; however, if you aim to keep the integration at its most simple, using only minimal sound event triggers, this can still be a fairly high-velocity environment in which sound can quickly be changed and played with in a malleable way, one which isn't at all concerned with final systems and efficient technical designs. The primary goal here, after all is to move quickly with ideas and get an immediate sense of what works and what doesn't, and most importantly to get a sense of what the experience will be for the player on the sticks. As with anything at this early stage, it is also very important to communicate to everyone involved, and at every review or test opportunity, that the sound and the implementation are at an early first-pass quality level, an L1 or L1.5 level, and that these sounds are to be considered throwaway placeholders, there for the purposes of learning what might feel good in terms of feature design feedback.

The choice of whether to do this work within the DAW or within the engine, or both, depends on a variety of factors. How fast do you need to move? Is the work required simply something that can be done to picture so that someone else can see it, hear it, and quickly provide a response to it? Is the work required to help a design team prototype the feedback for a feature? This could be a strategic combination of approaches that begins with a fast initial approval in a DAW sketch and then quickly moves into a super-rough, low-fidelity interactive prototype onscreen.

As a director, you may also be involved in a great deal of such concept meetings and pitches, leaving you very little time or bandwidth to implement sound in the engine itself, which is a great opportunity to work with the sound design, music design, or technical sound design team to have them either sit or work directly with the rest of the game designers and to integrate sound events and hookups, using a preliminary DAW sound design sketch as inspiration for the sound tone and style itself.

As always, continual communication is at the heart of this process and drives the work cycle. Perhaps one of the most important aspects of this work, as you may have already inferred, is the ability to hold ideas loosely and be open to exploring new things as they emerge, throwing out ideas and sounds that don't work, and exploring new or interesting design concepts and tones that are emerging as part of the collaborative process. This openness is at the heart of being a good collaborator, at the same time as being able to listen to and try out, the ideas and suggestions of others on the team. Suggesting and also trying out other ideas is a natural part of this creative exchange… getting excited about possibilities and being able to demonstrate through actual sound work some of yours or the team's early pillar ideas, and is a great way to become an integral and infectious co-creator inside the game or feature design process itself. This can be something that any member of the sound team should be capable of doing, and should be encouraged to jump in and participate in these early prototyping phases. I would even encourage, during the L1 sound phase, any sound designer to be able to even ignore any early direction or tonal work so far done by the director, as long as it allows them to be in the moment with the rest of the integration and exploration team, and explore ideas quickly with the goal of getting something working and executing on screen, all things must be made possible and allowable this early in service of a good idea. Any nudging back to the vision can, of course, be done later at the L2 stage, where a more identity-centric design pass becomes the focus of the work. But for those early stages, I would encourage complete and total freedom in being able to simply work alongside the team and try things out.

Pillars: Creative Project Pillars vs Production Pillars (And Owners)

Given that this process of achieving clarity is a continual process, we must also begin the process by finding some fundamental guiding creative pillars for the audio of the game that can be used as evaluation guides and ensure that the work is on the right track and resonating with the game's overall vision. These are often referred to as the audio pillars of the game direction, and this falls to the audio director, working closely with the game director and creative director, as well as other key directors to find audio pillars that resonate with the title.

It is important here to make a distinction between these initial creative audio pillars, which have to do with the overall vision of the entire game, and an often-used production term in which the work of various areas of responsibility is broken down into a variety of key sound 'pillars', or designated areas of responsibility. These production-centric pillar terms break down the sound into distinct areas of responsibility so that each area can have a pillar 'owner', usually at the senior or supervisor level, whose responsibility it is to own the work and implementation of each area – reviewing the work being done on each of those areas. This pillar ownership ensures that the area is on track from a content production and quality standpoint, has any risks flagged to production teams and the director, and also is reviewed and pre-approved as it goes into the game. There is usually a small team of sound designers working on each pillar under the guidance of the pillar owner.

The creative audio pillars, on the other hand, are overall direction and vision tools with which the audio director can discuss the vision of the title with either the sound team, or various other disciplines, and can push and pull the sound work during reviews based on these directorial pillars.

There are usually only two or three creative audio pillars on a project, as they need to be generally applicable as well as memorable. They also need to cover a very wide variety of contexts of the game, whether music, sound-based or dialogue-based, and especially be applicable to the overall mix of everything together. They will also often speak to the tone or style of the effect that the game wishes to have on its audience. Discovering these pillars is something that happens very early in the project, at the same time that the other disciplines in art, animation, and design are also working on finding their overall pillars. It makes sense to work with these other directors as part of that overall multidisciplinary team because the audio pillars will need to resonate strongly with the other department's visionary pillars. If worked on at the same time, it is often the case that some of the audio pillars can influence or inspire other disciplines, or even the overall vision of the creative director themselves. So, this can be an active and very participatory element of the audio director's early work in getting to know the team and the project.

Socializing and kicking the tires on these pillars is an essential part of this process. Presenting the initial pillars and getting the audio team, as well as the overall team's reaction and responses to them is a good way to see what resonates and what could potentially need to be tweaked.

Much of this work will also take place away from the game engine itself, with reference material gathered and made either directly in the DAW, or in the form of video clips and presentations that aim to show clearly what the audio pillars and overall design and effect of the game will be.

It should be stated here that these pillars can also be defined later, and in some cases an audio director is not brought onto the project until quite late in the development process, and they have to define the audio pillars at the same time as getting critical sounds into the game. Though not ideal, in these instances, with the majority of the other game discipline pillars already defined, it is likely to be fairly straightforward to take those existing creative pillars of art, design, animation, and quickly come up with audio pillars that resonate well with what is already established and understood to be working well for the overall direction of the game.

So, with the project creative pillars defined, presented, and widely understood, and sound production pillars each delegated to an owner, we can move forwards more confidently into development onscreen with our team.

Challenging Prevailing Narratives about Sound

It is another important impetus of an audio director, to challenge any underlying preconceived assumptions of the wider team members that audio is a post-production service that comes after the design and prototyping phase has been done. By being present at more early conception and strategic meetings, the audio aspect can be considered as an integrated part of the overall approach. The practical aspect of this allows audio teams to show rather than tell, which in early pre-concept or concept phases is always much more powerful in terms of impact on decision-making. By showing that audio can play a useful, proactive, and powerful partnership role in prototyping and design, early on, the rest of the team will begin to understand the value of early audio involvement, and begin to advocate to have audio present in the process.

Being a continual advocate on behalf of the audio design, is often what it takes in moving a team from thinking about audio as something that can be applied later on (the post-production, outsource mindset) and instead instinctively knowing that audio, as an iterative design partner, brings immediate impact to early ideation. This can help teams in any discipline understand their work from an onscreen practical dimension a lot earlier.

11 Technology, Production, and Information

Audio Pipeline Fluidity

A symptom of quick proof-of-concept implementation work is that it shows the need for more solid solutions to the problems at scale. The initial onscreen work will usually be rough and hacky, just to get the idea across and get a direction approved, but the actual feature work and content pipelines that will eventually be needed to support the work across the scope of the entire game is something that needs focus, time, and dedicated resources.

In more general terms, in the early stages of a project, focussing any audio technology tools and pipelines on allowing sound designers to very quickly iterate and integrate sound with low turbulence is an important initial stance during the (often lengthy) early phase of development. Working on solid, more advanced pipelines in these early phases may be premature, as the actual creative vision needs to take shape first.

Keeping the audio team's content flowing into the engine should be the priority. This is helped by the knowledge that once this phase of fluidity and creative uncertainty is over (or lessened), the real work of solidifying the technology features can begin. The result of this early tech environment should be that the content team can respond quickly when things change and the target moves. Solidifying too quickly, before the game loop is secured, and the tone of the game and the combination of its ingredients are known, potentially risks that a lot of architectural work will need to be undone and restarted, because big changes will continue to happen if the early exploratory phase has not achieved its goals of validating the experience.

This theme of leading with the creative work continues into the philosophy of tech and tools development beyond the early proof-of-concept phases. By having an audio team driven to produce the best creative and iterative work possible, this turns attention to your technology to provide fast iterative build pipelines, ideally in which sound content can be switched out or hot-swapped, while the game is still running.

DOI: 10.4324/9781003748465-12

This is a vision for audio technology. Reducing turbulence for the audio designers who are integrating work into the game is, for me, the number one priority for an audio technology team throughout production. This enables iterative gains, whether in the early L1 stages, or the later L3–L4 polish stages. Without this, any team will be challenged in achieving their creative goals due to technical turbulence. It not only needs visionary energy to lead such a technology approach, but practical energy to make sure that the desired outcome is achieved. Sound work also requires continual regression and maintenance work on the part of sound designers and integrators, as the upstream content continually adjusts to new benchmarks and new production requirements. Sounds that previously worked will continually break, so having an eye on solving this kind of regression, or re-conforming work, could also ensure that the team remains able to continue to deliver their work without becoming overwhelmed with rework.

Balancing Audio Teams

The modern audio development team is an ever-changing mosaic, a dynamic structure made of smaller pieces, coming together into an overall shape and then reshaping into new forms to meet ongoing changes in scale and scope. Getting the core audio team in place on any project is a huge challenge, whether this is a team you have inherited or is one you are building from the ground up. This is the team at the centre of the development process and will be the pieces of the mosaic that, while their roles may change, their presence and expertise at the centre of the game's development do not.

Who makes up the core internal in-house team members is worth spending a lot of time thinking about and working on. I would make the case for very proficient generalists or T-shaped people to be much better fits than specialists for a core team, given that the shape of the audio work on a dev team can change drastically on a day-to-day or week-to-week basis, and given that specialists usually only have a small area of production that they will need to be present for. Having a T-shaped person, a generalist with a deep specialization, also enables them to be able to develop deep expertise in one particular area, potentially owning that entire area as a pillar lead, all while the rest of the content support resources join to scale up around them.

Given the growth in external audio co-development resource options and teams globally, this gives you a lot of choice when it comes to building up a team for planned specialist and short-term work wherever the amount of content exceeds what the internal team can achieve.

Another way of establishing in-house roles is to look at the various areas of responsibility in each game and assign them to pillar owners. Having an in-house senior or supervisor on each of these pillars, at a larger double-A, triple-A, or quad-A scale, is critical in that the ownership and guidance of each of these areas can be fully given to those people as they work with the rest of the development team directly. The teams underneath each of those pillar owners can then be built up through either contractors, outsource co-dev teams, or other internal resources as the production may only need to reach maximum team size for specific periods of intense development. This enables the ownership and approval (accountability) to remain in-house. If more content work is needed to be achieved in a shorter amount of time, the amount of resources under the pillar owner may be scaled up. The pillar owner in those cases then begins to follow somewhat the responsibility path of the audio director, in that they need to surrender some hands-on duties and spend more time reviewing and approving the larger content team's work, giving clear feedback and ensuring that the right amount of iteration is taking place before the work is approved to an L3 final polish level according to the pillar vision.

So, when looking at in-house roles, as opposed to what roles can potentially be dynamically added through internal or external co-dev, the ability to which someone can step into this role of supervision and ownership, (with their feedback and people skills being either already developed well, or having a plan of action through which they can gain experience in giving this feedback and getting good results) needs to be considered. Any internal team members will have their growth areas presumably already mapped out, and the more time any audio designer can spend working on developing people skills, giving clear, actionable feedback in ways in which those receiving the feedback feel empowered to improve the work with each iteration, the better.

So, with the core in-house team members in place, we need to think carefully about leadership and responsibility overall, is there a need for a lead who sits between the audio director and the rest of the team? Or, in cases where you may be leaning away from being an audio director, or more into being a lead, is there a need for a more creative vision holder at the same level, or above the current leadership role that you hold, in order to enable you to focus on the technical side? Sketching all this out and running those plans and ideas through your trusted colleagues on the team will help get the best and most appropriate team size for your specific project.

Full-time internal hiring is always a serious undertaking and responsibility, it takes a lot of time, resources and it is a commitment to that person that they will be secure and taken care of by the audio team, the developer, and the larger company. In order to be able to genuinely make that commitment, you need rock-solid certainty that the role is critically necessary to be in-house and as close as possible to the development team on a day-to-day basis.

Contract sound designers as well as external co-dev partners can, in some cases, be deployed to come in and take the reins of a pillar, if a game explodes with much larger scope. However, there always needs to be a clear boundary that the accountability of the quality, and ultimate approval of the feature remains in-house with the developer.

Evaluation Processes

The ability for a team to bring in outside opinions on the sound is a critical part of the development process, as crucial as testing the game with playtest audiences.

You will have spent a lot of time collaborating with different disciplines and people on the team, balancing their thoughts and ideas with your own, trying out ideas, and working together to get something onscreen that fulfils the brief of the project and delivers for all those stakeholders. However, the true measure of whether or not the project is working onscreen, whether all those ideas, emotions, stories, and world-building elements are producing a desired overall entertainment experience, can only be validated when people outside of the team, and of course players, are exposed to the game and able to see it, hear it, and play it.

Most development teams have extensive user-testing and later on, playtests built into their production timelines and roadmaps as a validation and evaluation step, so that they can incorporate early feedback on the experience from perspectives outside of the team. In most cases, the audio portion of their experience will be measured as to how it contributes and affects the overall gameplay and story immersion experience, so sound, music, dialogue, and mix may only get minor mentions in any playtest feedback, and only if those elements stand out.

Receiving and teasing more detailed and nuanced audio feedback from play testers and general players can be a challenge on time and resources. In addition to which, the vocabulary to describe sound elements, such as frequency, timbre, mix layers, balance, clarity, and muddiness, are sometimes hard to find among general gaming audiences. So you may have to interpret feedback and comments written in a way that is quite different from anything you are used to reading.

In order to gather more targeted feedback, it requires the audio team to be able to reach out to a source of external feedback, so that they can get an objective, trusted, evaluation and to capture that valuable first impression of what the game sounds like to fresh ears.

For these trusted fresh ears, an audio director may reach out to various places. Depending on the team or corporate structure in which they find themselves, there may be other audio directors, or teams of centralized audio designers at the publisher level, who could be asked to take a listen to a particular section of a recent milestone, in order to gather audio-*specific* feedback.

To ensure this outreach is effective, making sure it is focussed and specific in its aims is important. There may be certain areas that the audio team is unsure of, and needs feedback on, so the game build, or game capture footage needs to be supplied along with specific questions and contexts communicated to the team listening, in order that their feedback can be focussed on the areas of interest. I always find it useful to leave in some very open questions when gathering external feedback, so that we can capture things that we may not be aware of at all. For example, two open-ended and easy questions along the lines of 'what is already working well?' and 'what are the opportunities for improvement?' may suffice to capture the most objective notes.

This is an important process as the audio team on a specific project is deeply focussed entirely on that project, and gets into the details of every sound, every feature, and every mix decision. This focus on the micro scale, can often hide what is happening at the much larger scale overall in the project. So, things like dialogue clarity, where the lines may be buried just enough that they are unintelligible to a first-time listener – are easy to capture in general feedback.

There is also a recency bias to putting new sounds into the game, in that those sounds are often mixed that little bit louder, whereas older, more familiar sounds are pushed to the back of the mix to make auditory room for those newer sounds. This is something that teams, while they work in the day-to-day, can be unaware of. Having objective feedback from a first-time player or listener, on what is clear and what is unclear, can be critical to understanding the overall big picture of what is working and what could be improved.

The other important element of this feedback-gathering process is that it absolutely has to be controlled and owned by the audio director. It cannot be something that is shared widely with the audio team as the team will likely just start to see every comment as an issue or task, and start to address all the feedback as though they were Jira tasks. It is critical that the audio director remains the decision-maker, the interpreter of the feedback, and is the person also commissioning the feedback, as well as receiving it *directly.* The step after receiving any commissioned feedback is in interpreting it for the team in the form of a clear presentation of the results, a breakdown of what will be addressed and what is fine to leave unaddressed, and the ensuing prioritized tasks responding to the feedback.

Remaining in control of the information that a wider audio team receives from any kind of audio review, is vitally important to the success of how well that feedback is implemented into the game. Sometimes you will get feedback but decide that there is no action required, or that the areas in question are simply something that you should keep an ear on as development progresses. Determining moments in production at which feedback can be given, for example, a first Vertical Slice, an Alpha build, or a Beta build are good ways to track progress and perception of any recurring issues that may have been identified.

Evaluations can also be used strategically at an executive level, for example, when a request for additional resources is desperately needed. Having outside objective expert opinions and feedback to back up those needs for resources can be critical to ensuring that it is not just the audio team's opinion that is being shown, it is an outside opinion that reflects what the audience thinks of the experience.

12 Overall Approaches towards Clarity

Clarity is a concept that sounds incredibly simple; just find the most important thing for the game experience and ensure that this comes through above everything else that may be going on in the game. At its most fundamental, as an overall north star, this is correct. However, the complexity and multifaceted nature of video games means that they can have a kaleidoscope of different elements, all working together to make up the overall experience. It is more likely that the most important concept for the game isn't just one thing, but a feeling or tone that is the result of a balance of several different ingredients working together over time.

Rather than thinking about the most important thing for the game's sound as a single, static element, the question has to be framed as dynamic. During reviews with the rest of the director team, figuring this out beat by beat, asking what is the most important thing for the player to feel and hear *in this moment,* is often the easiest way to understand the dynamic priorities and focal areas within your mix.

In video games, the mix is not a final production element of the game's sound that happens at the end, though there is a necessary period at the end in which the game must receive a final mix pass. The decision-making and structure all the way through development is how the mix is built from the ground up… understanding what the most important thing for a player to hear at certain moments is slowly revealed as the shape of the game experience itself is revealed. The mix must evolve as part of that process. The sooner you can start to ask these questions of dynamic importance, the sooner you can have a shape of the experience on screen, and be capable of tweaking and playing with that shape.

The Triangle of Sound

Any game sound (including music and dialogue) has three general forces pulling on it at any given moment. These three forces are ludic (or gameplay information for the player), the grounded world (or environmental believability),

DOI: 10.4324/9781003748465-13

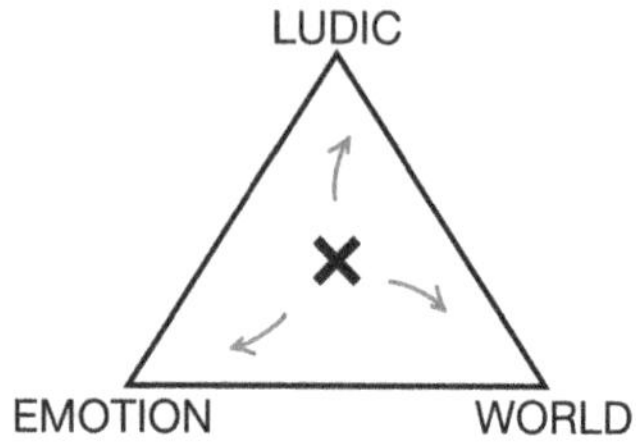

Figure 12.1 Triangle of sound image

and emotional (inner character Point-of-View (POV) elements of the sound, such as music or abstract sound design).

I have boiled this process down into a more interactive visual way of communicating with the rest of the team, in the form of the 'triangle of sound'. This can be a useful tool for expressing the vision of the overall experience with the team (Figure 12.1).

Achieving clarity means being able to foreground one of those three main elements of the sound of a game.

This may not be just one particular sound, but most likely a group of sounds. For example, in an important combat moment, the sounds the enemy is making may consist of the movement Foley, designed creature vocals, as well as designed effects of a special ability or attack. Yet the ludic information that the enemy is about to attack, and is charging up for that, is the most important element of sound at that particular moment, and all those sound ingredients can be foregrounded in the mix at that time.

With any foregrounding of sound, we naturally need to move the other elements to the background. So, if an emotional moment requires music and perhaps a vocalization to come to the foreground, then we naturally need to recede the environmental sounds, and some other ludic gameplay sounds into the background. This can be achieved with the dynamic mix, using perhaps a state or snapshot driven approach.

My biggest revelation here was about how to triangulate and ensure greater clarity by de-prioritizing those two background elements in terms of importance, so that one of them was still audible to a degree, and still able to be read by the audience if their attention was drawn to it. Put simply, you can only have one foreground and one background element, and not two background elements. So, it required the making of a choice, what element of the sound do we get rid of? Now, in mix terms this does not mean to turn the gain down completely, though in some cases this might be appropriate. This means that for mix decisions relating to clarity, you need to move the X *around the edges* of the triangle. Meaning that one element is always removed, or deprioritized, completely. This represents your decision-making of what to foreground and what becomes a secondary background element.

Any mix that attempts to get the X into the middle of the triangle is the worst possible mix because it is not making any decisions. In deciding not to remove something, the mix has no priority. What will result from this kind of mix is a muddy-sounding mess where everything feels like it is competing for the player's attention all the time. Flattening each element of the triangle at the same priority means that nothing is more important than any other element, and we have a mix that could essentially be just be done automatically by a compressor. *Direction* of the mix requires decision-making. Clarity requires decision-making.

The point here is that achieving clarity and finding the most important thing to emphasize in the game's sound is generally not any one single area, but a dynamic, constantly moving focus shift between foreground and background that creates an overall focussing effect. Discovering, through collaboration, what the focus needs to be at any given moment, forms the main backbone of the clarity process.

Mixing, still often one of the major afterthoughts of game audio, is to me the most direct expression of the game's design for the player, continually shifting, highlighting, and spotlighting what the player needs to hear, feel, or pay attention at any particular moment. It is the mix that is the most directly connected to expressing the dynamic shape of both the game design and creative direction itself, and ideally forms a continual, graceful, baton pass between information, realism, and emotion presented to the player. It is the overall expression of the entire experience. In the end, we should be able to draw a direct line from the game design, and any emotional story arc, to the mix in terms of what is important.

Knowing this, it becomes a priority for an audio director to understand the game design, building and modifying the shape of the mix as they work through all the various features, prototypes, sketches, revisions, and milestones, all the time understanding, with increasing clarity, as much as they can about the various shifting priorities of what the player needs to hear as they move through the game.

Natural Forces

The triangle can also be used in a non-mix context to help with direction for either sound design, music, or dialogue. It is a useful visual representation of where the emphasis needs to be for each element. In the opposite way to how the mix needs us to move the X position around the edges of the triangle (in order to make a decision to remove one element at a particular moment) the iterative *design* process for sounds themselves more naturally moves towards the centre of the triangle.

While sound, music, and dialogue all tend to have elements of the three forces demanded of them, pulling them more towards the centre of the triangle, each area also has a fundamental core identity or role to perform.

Music is primarily an emotional sound element. ('what our emotions sound like')

Sound is primarily a world element. (the 'language of nature', believability, a sense of groundedness)

Dialogue is primarily an informational element. (our clearest way to receive instructions and precise information)

Given that these three areas most naturally occupy each of those three corners of the triangle, you can see why it may offer some interesting strategies for a creative director to play against these.

We may insist on a 'single origin' approach, perhaps for the importance of clarity, that each of those three areas primarily occupy their most resonant corners of the triangle, leaving no ambiguity or uncertainty about what role each is performing, and optimizing each corner with its own distinct food group to do that work.

Similarly, we may decide that this is too obvious and on-the-nose for the kind of game being made, and we will lean into more emotional elements for the dialogue, more world building and groundedness for the music, and more informational roles for the sound effects. Effectively switching their primary roles. Perhaps emotional for the sound design, informational for the music, and believability of the world for the dialogue. Switching the primary corner of each of the food groups gives us some interesting creative lenses for direction and playing with expectations.

In the same sense, and this is mostly how many directors work today, we may focus on iterating and refining elements of every food group to do slightly different things, in a more 'blended' approach to the direction of food groups. So, some music cues may be acting as emotional core cues, others may be primarily informational and ludic state cues, while others may be operating as pure world-building musical cues. Similarly in dialogue or sound design, certain lines may be purely emotional, while others are informational and others are there simply to solidify the believability of the world, and so on.

So, using the triangle of sound as a way of making and communicating mix decisions about the game, moving around the edge of the triangle and staying away from the middle for this purpose can be a great help in terms of establishing clarity with the wider team and help with onscreen decisions. Similarly, using the same triangle to relate to individual *design* elements, music cues, dialogue lines, or sound effects, when giving feedback to a composer, actor or sound designer, means being able to play with the balance of the design against those three forces at play on every sound in the game.

13 Directing the Team

Reviews and Punchlists

Throughout all of the work on the team, being able to review the work against the lenses of the creative game audio pillars remains a central role of an audio director. Giving feedback and guidance on each particular review where adjustment or opportunities to push further are evident. Audio director reviews are where these craft-focussed review sessions usually happen. This can be either a live review, with the team and a producer present to take notes and assign tasks to the punchlist, or it can be a review that happens with the audio director making a playthrough of the game, capturing that playthrough as a video, and then reviewing the playthrough video making specific notes for the team to address in the form of a document or list. This can then later be turned into trackable, assignable tasks for the team by a producer later.

This review list often takes the form of a review punchlist. This is a list of notes that are prioritized accordingly from P1, P2, P3 to P4 priorities, P1 being the highest and P4 the lowest. This way anyone receiving these notes as tasks knows that the P1 tasks must be worked on first, then moving to the P2s, and then to the P3s. The priority designation is important because it helps the assignee understand that if time is short, then they know which tasks are the most important. There also exists a P0 designation, which is a 'drop everything and do this task before the end of the day' – this one is often required during director reviews where the team needs to get to a particular quality bar for a very specific deadline, such as a public demo or a vertical slice milestone that will be played and evaluated by senior executives. These reviews make progress only by having their punchlist items addressed from each review ready for the next day's review, ensuring that progress is made only in the areas that are called out in those reviews.

Director reviews that generate punchlists override the usual work of whatever a sound team may be working on. If they are working towards content or getting certain features to work, a director's punchlist will take precedence.

This kind of review or demo build of a game often happens on a separate branch of the development build version control software, so while the main

DOI: 10.4324/9781003748465-14

team continues with their work over on another branch, the polish and punchlist review tasks can be worked on separately.

The punchlist is an incredibly useful and important tool for a director to be able to prioritize and focus the work of the team at certain crucial times during development.

Relational Dynamics (Connecting Small Details to Big Picture)

Direction and vision necessitate all kinds of fascinating perspectives and approaches to working on sound. In the processes of reducing a game direction, and subsequently the audio direction, to easily communicable overall gestures, we also need to consider how our game, or games, relate to the overall landscape of other games, and by further extension how they relate to the landscape of overall entertainment within the current context that the game is being released into.

This overall context is one of both a cultural and marketing landscape that has been constructed and engineered to push certain game and entertainment genre elements to the foreground. In a sense, every piece of entertainment is jostling to stand out and grab attention. This is done, in part, through various kinds of categorization and genre blending. Codifying the game as having a certain genre or tone is a shortcut to triggering the antennae of fans of other genres and Intellectual Property that already exist in this continuum. Sound, music, and voice play a massively important role in this identity and branding. It is the wider cultural entertainment context in which our thinking is shaped when we try to articulate our audio principles or pillars as lenses through which we are able to evaluate the work that is occurring on our projects. What experiences do our games offer, and how might a player engage with that experience over the course of a day or week? Considering sound from this much wider perspective can be a good practice.

This is all quite far away from the things that probably led us here in the first place, which is the craft of designing sounds that fit with a visual image, gameplay sequence, or feature, and feel compelling and satisfying to interact with. This process; the discovery, the decision-making, the iteration and refinement processes, the reaction of others to the work, and incorporation of feedback and suggestions, all of this comes together as the satisfying and creative work of interactive audio design.

It is the realization that all of these daily and hourly efforts need to fit into an overall cohesive whole that eventually becomes a bigger picture. I think we all feel, after some time of working on content, that there are undiscovered and unanswered questions about how all of this work fits into a bigger cohesive whole, or package. And so, this leads you, from small details, to discovering as much as you can about the level, map, and eventually the overall project as you can. This then leads you to finding out where this game fits inside the oeuvre of work overall at the studio, and then beyond the studio to competitive games and titles, and then beyond that into the entertainment sphere to include movies, television, and other forms of entertainment. The thirst for context, where does our work fit in? What does it mean? Is there an opportunity to stand out, to do things differently at certain moments, to establish some bigger and wider pattern of impact on the whole overall picture? We can very quickly go from thinking about a small sound and then pull out into this wider world of contexts, and then back in again. Perhaps this urge to stand out and to have an impact, or make a ripple in that broader entertainment pool, is in some way a need for our work, to have meaning – that it not be something worthless that in the end nobody gets to experience. This is a paradox that we deal with on every title we work on, every sound and piece of code that we work on; the possibility that the game may not find an audience, it may not get to the point of being released into the world, as so many projects are, unfortunately, fated to be cancelled at various stages of production.

Whether the work reaches an audience of millions, or whether it is only played by a few people, or perhaps only ever experienced by the team making it, is on some level irrelevant. The process of the work itself is, and to me should be, satisfying enough – anything that happens afterwards is out of your control anyway – whether an audience engages with the work, resonates with it, that is not for you to decide. Whether your title sells tens of millions of copies, or isn't even released, the fact remains that it is the work that you are here for – the craft, the day-to-day, the team, and the various rhythms and cycles within that process of discovery. What a beautiful thing it is we get to do in the world of interactive game development – each day working and crafting, refining and reshaping something that can be put into the hands of another person and experienced by them as an entire world! To play any role in that kind of process is a gift, all of us on every team being individual craftspeople of various kinds, all helping to put that world on screen.

As a director, feeling alive to these kinds of connections where the eventual work will be experienced, and in what contexts, is something we need to be able to be open to as fully as we can, and to use that as a signal with which we can enthuse and inspire our teams – helping connect *them* with that same feeling and understanding of overall context – to help everyone understand that their role in the creation of a project has meaning – whether it ships or not.

Maybe I've zoomed out a little too far here, but this is certainly how I feel when I experience music or cinema that resonates with me – those experiences are deeply personal and go beyond the work of all the individuals who worked on them – what those creators have done is to build something together as a team, and put it out into the world. Games are no different, in fact they may be even more potent worlds and experiences for an audience's imagination. Once an audience engages with that, the experience has a life of its own, it becomes a personal experience that each and every person experiencing it has completely to themselves.

A painter working on a canvas has this relational process of doing just that, working overall, then zooming in to add detail, then out to add something else, balancing and tweaking all the time, in and out, full image to small area. This kinetic action of relational dynamics, scaling in and out, is the same process for sound designers, composers, and dialogue designers… continually seeking updated relational information about the overall picture in which the music cue, the sound event, ambience, or the dialogue lines sit, in order to better ensure that the small individual components are what they need to be.

A director's role is very much relational in this way, to understand this overall context of the entire game, including all the elements and food groups of sound, music, dialogue, and mix, working together to articulate a singular effect that will be experienced by a player.

The degree to which you need to employ relational dynamics when discussing a feature or a single sound's context, will vary, but referring it always to the wider contexts in which it sits, levels above which the sound designer is working, can be a necessity for clarity. Often a designer can be working without wider contexts, with someone working so exclusively in one area of responsibility that they do not necessarily consider where or how their work will sit within the overall context. This will always result in a readjustment.

This lack of context can often be referred to as 'siloed' work or behaviour. Ambience is a great example here, as I can think of many examples of pillar owners going deep into details and features that are so intricate and time-consuming that they start to become akin to real-world environments with seasons, cycles, incredibly realistic reverb and distance modelling and so on. Understanding the context in which each ambience will be experienced by the player is critical to informing the degree to which detail needs to be present. A step back to view gameplay examples happening in various world locations may well reveal that, for example, during combat, all of the ambience needs to get out of the way so that the combat experience and informational sound related to that combat is clearly readable and understandable to the player. This is fine if your game is a balance of world exploration and combat, but if your game starts to lean much more into the ludic aspects of combat, to the point that exploration and experiencing the ambiences only goes as far as being a transition into the next combat event, then ambiences need to be little more than a brief transition element, so the effort, the technology, the content, and the detail, can be scaled back to fit those contextual needs. This frees up bandwidth; from a technical memory viewpoint, to a creative and production bandwidth viewpoint. I'm conflicted whenever I hear this in a game, where something fleeting and barely noticeable in the overall experience has been given extreme polish and attention, sometimes this can be amazing, but on the whole, I would rather the polish and attention go into the areas that the player is going to spend the most time with, and that they are going to appreciate more over time.

Early, Mid and Late Creative Fuel

Prior to receiving pillars, there may be opportunities with which you can strengthen your creative options and lenses by capitalizing on a period in which there are no frames or guidance already in place. Any inspiration can fuel sketches in any direction at all, and these can be stored or kept on standby in case an opportunity for those ideas to be brought forward as options and propositions should arise. This is also a good opportunity to explore ideas between projects.

Everyone on the team can participate and partake in this kind of approach, where there is no brief in place, or work towards an invented brief to quickly generate a lot of sound material.

One reason for doing this kind of fast and far exploratory work is that the creative ideas and fuel that occur on first contact with a new idea can be extremely potent, as they are completely open to the interpretation of the person creating them. As mentioned, this initial propulsion and exploration of ideas can occur whenever a sound designer first sees a new piece of concept work, or hears a new idea or proposal. What occurs in the mind of the designer will naturally be something that is full of possibilities and resonances with their own tastes and preferences. Quickly exploring these territories is the goal of this kind of exercise.

I would highly encourage this kind of open exploration based on imagined briefs, but certainly this will require some form of time-boxing before the fuel of inspiration runs out – the impetus for sketching and putting down ideas in this 'new' idea state can also run out very quickly, after which it may be time to move on to something much more brief-oriented and focussed.

This method can also be used strategically at any time in a project; if a team or a particular team member is flagging creatively, they may need some time in which to completely focus on other material in order to refresh, so that they may return more invigorated. Figuring out the ways in which this new burst of creative energy can be re-deployed back into a project with already exhausted and depleted creative opportunities is a good challenge for a team.

"The Secret"

Another creative technique is called the sound designer's secret. This is a technique whereby an audio director, or creative director, gifts a secret to the sound designer that will change the underlying subtext about everything they do – the idea being that they can never tell any of the other team members about this secret. It is a kind of 'spoiler' technique that only works if nobody else knows the information. Knowing about a hidden subtext, or a secret reveal, is something that allows a sound designer to work from deep inside of the sound design outwards.

To give an example, if we are working on a particular character or creature enemy sound design palette, and it is a huge terrifying creature, filled with rage and anger, extremely dangerous, and must appear to the player as the most terrifying creature they will encounter in the game. There is a need to ramp this up in the design so that it is something special. We are not thinking of the mix here, because undoubtedly with this kind of brief, there is a lot that needs to be done with the mix in order to foreground this creature and its importance in the sound field, but we focus on the design components and elements only.

The secret I will reveal to the sound designer in charge of this creature is that it is actually a creature that spends most of its life-cycle in a completely different form, in fact a very furry, loving and playful form, and is extremely loving and family focussed – what has happened here is that it has lost its young child, and is desperately trying everything it can to find that child and return back home.

Immediately, from within this idea, we can start to colour in some of the missing emotional elements, what would it sound like when it is with its family, in its own home environment, what kind of baseline are we operating from… from there, we can build an idea of just how angry, how painful, how the emotion and energy is bursting out from within, from every fibre of its being calling to its child. We need the designer here to channel much of this intensity and emotion from within the creature, making it connect personally where we can, getting a more empathetic approach, which will ultimately connect with the audience too.

The hidden subtext that we provide can be anything that is true in the story and yet to be revealed, or it can be world building that is never actually revealed in the story, but is something that is invented as a way of further developing the emotional subtext of the world. Because sound design is itself a form of subtext that cannot literally be read as pure information by someone else, we can weave and elaborate on these kinds of textures and sub-stories in order that our team can push the emotional design elements far further than they perhaps would have if they were simply designing for what they see on the surface.

This technique is also often used in music direction, when a director is discussing the subtext and emotional feeling of the score with a composer, they will often connect immediately to the 'big emotional idea' of the game. And this is very often something that the director wants to keep very close to themselves, and may not actually share with the rest of the team. They can treat this very much as a deep secret for the project, in order to get a particular tone under the image.

It can be the case that if everything lines up, the onscreen visual style, the animation style, the music style, the sound design style and the dialogue, then we, as audiences, are left with no ambiguity and nothing to interest us.

There are no mysteries, there is nothing for us that is unknown about what we are experiencing, nothing to make us think we need to go emotionally deeper into this world. This is when music Mickey-Mouses the onscreen. For music, when Mickey-Mousing for example, this would essentially be doing the job that Foley and sound design are already doing, embodying and grounding the character onscreen. This is when we can say that something is too 'on-the-nose'. On the contrary, when visuals and sound point in different directions, an entire universe of ambiguous time and space can be opened up for the audience, and we become hungry for further exploration into the stories and the world.

I was told about many subtexts on *Shadow of the Tomb Raider* by our creative director, which I won't reveal here, but that felt so contrary and at the same time a complimentary to the adventure line, that they resonated underneath. Musically, it felt like we were scoring an entirely different story to the one onscreen. The subtext line and adventure line were running simultaneously, but the subtext was, and could never be, something that could be obviously read and understood by the audience. It was always a 'secret' that the audience could feel, but never be explicitly aware of.

Technical Distractions

At some point along the way, direction, for me, has moved to where I spend very little time thinking directly about the under-the-hood 'audio' details of sound design, dialogue or music. The technical vernacular of audio in particular is increasingly isolating in communicative and creative terms, especially in collaboration with other disciplines, which is where most of my work as a director occurs. Audio language does not accommodate anything beyond quite literal and objective description of the frequencies and technical features of the sound itself. Creative and directorial conversations concerning the vision revolve around pacing and emotional feel, and to this end, I may need to translate some of this into audio language for an audio team, though this is also part of a collaborative conversation as we work to solve creative problems together.

More often than not, someone making a big deal about those technical features of the sound can actually be unable to tell the difference between the A/B comparison, when taken away from the metering, spectrograms and waveforms… the differences being so subtle as to be imperceptible in most cases. Direction-wise, talking about how a sound fits within the triangle of needs, and how much of each of those forces the sound needs to appease is always a more fruitful conversation for me. The vernacular of audio and the way the overall sound is shaped I will leave to the eventual, and continual, mix conversations. Plug-ins and plug-in marketing have increasingly exaggerated the importance of audio-speak, underneath which I believe is this overall psychological suggestion of 'control' over sound, as though it were the compression, saturation, and transient shaping that gives sound meaning to an audience.

No, if we have a review meeting about sound between myself and a sound designer, we will most often not be talking in audio vernacular. We will instead be talking about feeling, the context, the pacing, ideas of contrast, the space, the focus, foreground, background, whether a sound needs to be diffuse or precise, the arc and shape of the overall sound style and perspectives, and where all these small bits and pieces might fit into the overall big picture. Overall shape, as well as clarity and ambiguity.

In the same way that a collaborative conversation with an engineer, audio or otherwise, will not involve me focussing on talk of code and the efficiency of any system, or digging into the syntax and sub-routines to express some tiny (important) detail, my role will be to clearly state the desired outcomes onscreen of that particular feature or moment – listen to the various proposed solutions, and make decisions based on any questions that come up to challenge the initial idea. In fact, it is this conversation that can be the most rewarding and exciting, to have someone who thoroughly sees and understands the solution architecturally and is able to question the vision from a completely different perspective.

All Sound is Relative

Any sound can have its meaning completely changed by what is being heard at the same time above or below it (harmonic context), or beforehand or afterwards (sequential context). Being able to direct the overall experience onscreen means being aware of this axis of interrelationships.

Sequential context gives us a shape, a path, a line which we follow and read as auditors. Is a sound getting louder the more we head in a certain direction, or is there a repetition or variance to sounds heard in sequence, suggesting either a mechanical or natural source? There are many aspects to these kinds of temporal sequential contexts that can be manipulated to convey different information, tell different stories, and fulfil narrative or character arcs.

Harmonic context, that of sounds being heard while another sound also plays as a supporting or background element, is another such relational element. A baby crying while a spring-like ambience full of life also plays can reinforce an overall effect of this being a joyful moment. With the sound of wind and dust blowing in the ambience, rather than birds, we give a different feeling, a different harmonic context. The sound may be the exact same, but the other sounds that we hear around it, in relation to that sound, give completely different effects that can be used to tell different stories and create different moods.

Working to get this overall relational meaning and emotional information to line up and convey the feelings needed by the game becomes a primary focus of direction work.

If we explore and talk about the world element of the triangle of sound, and how grounded the sound might need to feel, we may get into some of the technical aspects of how the sound could play. But, again, the purpose of this is to convey a particular effect, rather than thinking too much about how that effect is achieved through whatever kinds of processing. As directors, we need to be able to focus on whether or not the sound feels convincing or not, and to be able to articulate what elements may be hindering or delivering that believability. So, the role as director here is not to get too much into the 'how'; that is, for the designer to have ownership and control over, it is to be able to articulate and explain the 'why' and to be able to clearly articulate when the criteria for the 'why' is being met.

Motivation: The Continual Improvement of Project, Team, and Environment

At some point, we start to understand that all the problems we are helping to solve form a part of some general overall vector of continual improvement. For instance, if we are unable to play back or check sounds into the build, we are focussed on collaborating with programmers and engineers on solving those issues. Once solved, we become focussed next on speeding that process up from hours to minutes. From there we are solving other issues, and as we gradually ease each frictional issue, we shift focus onto addressing new problems. Once technical barriers are removed, we move to designing the sound so that the effect serves gameplay, perhaps the emotional impact, or to conveying some kind of groundedness (weight, distance, density, material) and feedback on elements from the game world. All so we may be able to face each new request or issue from the team in a reasonably time-sensitive way with some sense of stability.

There may be personality or political issues that also need to be resolved on the team, where colleagues are working contrary to the overall goals of the team, for example, by foregrounding needs of specific disciplines over those of the game itself. Audio can be as guilty as anyone else on the team of this.

There is always something to do and something that can be improved. Some nuance to this, of course, is possible, as certain people may focus more on managerial elements of this continual improvement, helping with specific legal or practical matters; unblocking the team (for example, music licensing, or sourcing external audio teams). We may end up developing tools and techniques that can be applied far further than a single project, across multiple projects and teams. Tool and pipeline development has been a major trend within the industry since the beginning – attempting to accelerate the integration of sound into game engines and have it been as pain-free and iterative as possible, so that the audio designers themselves may focus more on the actual 'design' problems of the work.

We may think of these as primary, secondary and tertiary problems. Technology and pipelines are a primary problem, because without this, you cannot even play, replace, or tweak a sound in the game.

Design problems are a secondary problem, in that the sounds being created and implemented need to give the player a variety of critical information about gameplay; enemy health, waypoints, objectives, progress on particular tasks and so on. Whereas tertiary problems could be thought of as aesthetic issues, relating to identity, story, character point-of-view, and the 'feel' of a sound or haptic design. These layers of problem solving roughly correspond to our notions of quality L-levels, in that we build the sound for a game up in these same layers, solving these problems in order of importance, building upon each previous layer as a foundation.

Outside of these project-related problems are the cultures and rituals within our team and development environment that enable us to get to the important part of actually doing the work. Fair compensation, working hours that are sustainable for the long term, a team environment where people feel valued, and in which their work is meaningful, where they can have creative opportunities to explore and deliver on the ideas of the team. All of the systems, checks and balances that are necessary for the culture to support the employee, rather than giving them more problems. Management and leadership here in this latter context are about being a supporter of the team, available to help resolve problems, be a sounding board for ideas, offer fresh ears on reviews, brainstorming and helping resolve whatever issues the team, or individual team members, may be experiencing.

Continual improvement then, is a sum total of what motivates us to continue working each day. We have short-term improvements for the day or week, mid-term goals for the month or year, and long-term goals for the project or technology cycle, and perhaps even far longer-term goals and visions for the five to ten years beyond, of what the work and world of sound for games could look and feel like.

Continual Improvement: Wider Industry

This drive for continual improvement must also by nature apply to the more general and far wider environmental ecosystem in which our own studios and projects sit – that of the industry as a whole.

As we share techniques, tools, pipelines, and novel solutions more widely and publicly via conferences, articles, video tutorials, podcast conversations, and interviews, the overall circulation of ideas and techniques flows throughout the industry.

Change is a constant for all of us. Shifts in technology, in culture, in economic conditions, and in the way we make games and the kinds of games we make are all inevitable. Responding to those changes, seeing opportunities, perhaps making some leaps into new possibilities can lead to breakthroughs that can ripple across the industry, shared first with our closest teams, and eventually the industry as a whole.

Traits of Triage

A term we hear a lot in game development is 'triage', in particular when it comes to production and bug fixing. This approach is also used more widely in game development around the time of major milestones, where time and resources become limited to what can be achieved using the available resources. This is also how prioritization of tasks and bugs is achieved.

The definition of triage comes to us from battlefield conditions and their medical responses, and was later introduced into mainstream hospitals in the 1960s where the sorting and allocation of treatment to victims according to a system of priorities – designed to maximize the number of survivors – brings a calm logic to a deeply stressful environment.

After some deeper research into the origins of this term, I made note of a few different descriptions of what traits make a good triage nurse, which match so well to the traits of an audio director on a project that they are worth listing here for inspiration.

Personal Traits:

Flexibility
Autonomy
Effective communication
Assertiveness
Patience
Compassion
Willingness to listen and learn

Behavioural Traits:

Applies intuition
Confidence in judgement
Works well under pressure
Organized
Able to improvise
Trust in, and reliance on, peers

Cognitive Traits:

Ability to prioritize
Uses critical thinking
Able to make decisions quickly
Diverse knowledge base
Knows when not to act

For me, this reads very closely to a list of ideal attributes for an audio director, particularly when finalizing a game to get it across the finish line. And how wonderful would it be to see a job description that listed even some of these areas. Of course, in game development, the stakes are not nearly as high as in a medical emergency, yet the method by which priorities are sorted and assigned remains relevant for prioritizing the overall experience of the player.

Spatial Visions

Visions for games need not only apply to the sound design, the dialogue, the music, and the mix, but also now to the dimensionality of the space of the game.

Approaches to the readability of the 3D space of a game world are relatively new areas to have to deal with.

For a distinctively creative Dolby Atmos mix, *Cairn*, a survival climber game, is a wonderful example. A kind of narrative-driven rock-climbing simulator, the player must control and place the hands and feet of climber Aava to conquer the various faces of the fictional Mount Kami.

The game has a distinctive Atmos mix, with very careful thought placed on what exactly is panned to and included in what speaker, with particular attention to the overhead channels for height sounds. With wind being a key feature of the game's soundscape, it is important that there isn't too much masking of other positional sounds. One of the decisions that is the most interesting, from a spatial fidelity standpoint, is the decision to only include sounds in the overheads that emphasize height or that signal things above the player, like bird calls or some of the 3D sounds from flapping flags. When soloing the overhead channels, we hear only these 3D sounds and none of the ambient wind sounds. These detailed surround sound winds are crafted in 7.1 and remain anchored to those lower channels as the camera is panned around. The overall effect of this decision to exclude winds from the height channels is a preservation of the vertical effects of the sound, as well as adding to the clarity and readability of the game environment. This is an altogether clever aesthetic decision, as most Atmos mixes intuitively want to pan all the diegetic sounds in all channels, at all times.

In analysing and listening to many Dolby Atmos mixes, we can learn much about the various different approaches to bring creativity into the spatial realm. The movie *Apocalypse Now*, interestingly, is also now available in an Atmos mix format, and given the incredible provenance of the sound and the mix in that film, I was expecting to hear all kinds of sounds being panned around and into the overhead space. However, we find a refreshing and extremely limited approach to the height channels – we have a mix that faithfully preserves, for the most part, the 7.1 mix from previous versions of the film, and only in one or two scenes is any sound at all panned to the height channels. One scene where the Tannoy sound of a helicopter searching for a stolen surfboard can be heard, is sourced overhead, as though it is really above the audience. There is also one brief moment in the jungle, when Chef is looking for mangoes, but instead discovers a tiger, that we hear some of the insects and jungle sounds in advance of that tiger attack moment start to wrap around the audience in the height channels – immersing them audience further in this environmental jungle moment.

These more minimal and subtractive approaches to the overhead height channels give inspiration for new approaches. Not just panning every 3D sound up to the height channels for the sake of it, but carefully choosing what to include and what to exclude. The 3D space becomes one for creative staging, not just for the automated inclusion of all diegetic sound.

To use another example from outside of games, in Dolby Atmos music mixes (examples can be found and listened to through Apple Music, or similar spatial music streaming platforms), a medium freed entirely from the moving image, where you would expect complete freedom from the musical 'stage' in front of the listener, there are very few examples of the use of height or surrounds to send separate information, the majority instead choosing to create a static sound stage on which the music is heard from the 'front', with reverbs adding the barest suggestion of live space to the surrounds and height channels. The effect of which is to widen the acoustic space as though to mimic the perception of hearing the music from a theatre seat within an acoustic environment.

Perhaps understandably there is emphasis on Left and Right channels to carry the main instruments and vocals, and also very often an under-used centre channel. This staging effect is generally disappointing for such a new creative medium freed from the concept of a screen, though there are a few examples where spatialization is approached more creatively, with the separation of distinct instruments. Bjork's *Cornucopia: Live* is a fantastic example of creative spatialization of the sound field. It really separates sound, instruments, and vocals, and treats the idea of a sound stage more theatrically. As mentioned, when freed from having any kind of visual elements on which to attach sounds as a source, music is spatially free to move anywhere, and to represent anything, On the opening track, 'Family (Intro)', when the vocal comes in towards the second half, we hear this panned exclusively into the top front overhead channels, which makes a clear statement that you are listening to something different. Games too can learn a lot here; instead of playing it safe, panning 3D sound where expected, there are new techniques and possibilities for amplifying the spatial and immersive effects of the format.

Preserving and even exaggerating spatial vertical fidelity, so that height can clearly be 'read' by an audience, is a key experience of Atmos mixes. It is far too easy with myriad sound sources moving around the player, to quickly have spatial effects become overwhelming, leading to incoherence. By choosing to think more carefully and strategically about what to include in the overheads, the game Cairn shows an exciting way forward for spatial mixes. This is bold and confident use of the options and choices available with 3D space, and shows a clear understanding of the masking effects of ambient sound against the spatialization effect of height.

14 A Studio Director Perspective

Studio Audio Direction/Head of Audio

As we exhaust the possibilities of audio direction for a single project, up at the highest level of the hierarchy of responsibilities, at least within the audio craft group, we find the 'studio audio director' or 'head of audio' for a particular studio group or publisher. This is an organizational node that is accountable for and oversees a large group of studios working across multiple different titles. Each of those titles will have an audio director working with their own creative audio pillars and teams. So, what focus might a studio audio director or head of audio have?

The Centre of Craft Excellence (CCE)

To be useful to the teams that are being served, the studio audio director is usually tasked with an overall approach to define and promote craft excellence for the studios. Ensuring that quality, processes, and best practices are in place and that the projects are all continuing to be run well, and that the results onscreen meet the (clearly defined) quality bar of the studio group. This is a strategic role established to see overall advantages, efficiencies, and resonances that help all the Audio Directors and projects. At this high level, mandating too much, pulling everyone to the middle will create a sense of sameness, whereas staying towards the edges, but still within the circle of general support, creates a sense of belonging at the same time as embracing individuality on each title.

All centres of craft excellence are created differently to respond to the shape of the organization they support, but they usually fall into three broad approaches in scale. It is often best to think of them as being built from the top down, starting with the highest levels of accountability of audio, via some overall evaluation responsibilities.

High-Level CCE (Evaluations)

At the highest level, a CCE can operate by evaluating all the projects currently in development at regular milestones. Evaluation can take several forms, but

DOI: 10.4324/9781003748465-15

the most meaningful is a regular, formalized, objective audio review expressed in the form of a report of the onscreen quality of the game. Feedback here is usually centred on specifics; a review of the current milestone build, taking detailed notes upon which an overall executive summary is based. This summary at its most minimal articulates for the executive leadership team any craft areas that are working really well, and any areas where there are opportunities for improvement. This report can then be considered as part of any general evaluation processes that a publisher takes part in. These reviews are often called a 'green-light process' or a gated review. Providing continual and trackable evaluation on a title in development, action items from these reviews mean that progress can be measured on any areas that need to be addressed. It is a critically important moment when a project can be green-lit to continue, or stopped on conditions, or halted altogether.

As an opportunity to review titles in development, this is an ideal place to employ sound principles as lenses for each area of an evaluation; Sound, Music, Dialogue, and Mix. This is in addition to the consideration of whether the project is clearly expressing and hitting its own stated creative audio pillars, which should be understood before any evaluation or review can take place.

Expectations of the quality bar for the group, and the communication of those expectations is a critical function of this high-level CCE. Understanding the benchmark and pushing teams to exceed it becomes a combination of communication, strategizing, coaching, and assisting.

Further evaluation may take the form of some more overall health signifiers, and a deeper dive may be made into the production plans of the project, as well as its priorities, measuring technology stack frictions (time taken to get a sound onscreen), creative pillars, and overall communication health. Consideration may be given to a wide suite of factors, such as the breakdown below that looks at summarizing the technical, creative, and collaborative health of various projects in development at the publisher level (Figure 14.1).

Mid-Level CCE (Supervision, IC Craft Expertise, Production, Management)

Once the high-level accountability and evaluation functionalities have been established, the CCE can next turn to building a layer of highly experienced craft excellence resources who can be assigned across various projects as needed. Having people who are able to jump in and help out on projects does two things. Firstly, it concentrates and develops a huge amount of audio expertise, giving centralized resources exposure across multiple projects within a relatively short space of time. This also exposes them to multiple ways of approaching solutions to similar problems, and with this comes the ability for them to optimize and circumvent problems from one team to another with tried and tested repeatable approaches.

Example Project Evaluation Ratings

SUMMARY TABLE OF ALL PROJECTS

	Project 01	Project 02	Project 03	Project 04	Project 05	Project 06	Project 07
Technical Rating	C	A	B	B	AA	D	C
Creative Rating	B	A	C	B	A	D	D
Collaborative Rating	A	AA	D	AA	A	C	D

Ratings Legend	
AA	Exemplary
A	Minor Improvements & Tweaks
B	Some Remediation Opportunities
C	Need Remediation Plan
D	Time-Critical Remediation Plan & Action

Each rating and IMPROVEMENT PLAN is based off a variety of factors. Via a regular Report.
Technical Rating: Tools, Pipelines, Access to Programming Support, Time to iterate. Amount of time sound team spends building, debugging, working around problems (frustration), tech request list health, Amount of technical turbulence & change etc
Creative Rating: Quality & understanding of Vision Pillars & Supporting Material, Creative Review Process, Excitement Level of Team, Impact / buy-in of vision on other disciplines. On-the-sticks reviews of audio.
Collaborative Rating: Proactivity of Audio Communication (team-wide show & tell presence etc), Audio Integration into Production Planning Materials & Presentations, Production Awareness of Audio, Integration into feature Cells, Art, Design Integration of Audio Team et al. Trust level of leadership in audio. Amount of audio teams involved.

Figure 14.1 Example of CCE health evaluation snapshot of several projects in development

The other thing is that it gives the projects access to deeply experienced talent that can drop in whenever needed. The bigger the group of studios being supported, the deeper this bench of talent can be.

The mid-level of a CCE carries senior craft experts who are able to design and integrate sound directly themselves, operating as leads, senior supervisors, principal sound designers, technical sound designers (building shared tools and systems), or even occasional stand-in directors on projects that may need this kind of assistance. Their seniority will increase rapidly due to the number of projects they become exposed to.

In addition to these senior resources, expert craft managers and producers can also be put in place in a similar way to move between projects that need additional organizational assistance at various moments during their production.

This bench of centralized talent can help with the remediation plans of any studio evaluation, and form a cohesive and effective plan to help projects get where they need to be in order to ship on time and at the expected quality bar.

Low-Level CCE (IC Contributors)

At the lowest level, this is the most hands-on in terms of type of work, and it is here we may see even more centralized sound designers, dialogue designers, or music designers and implementers, as well as technical sound designers. Similar to the mid-level, these resources can be full-time and also move around a lot from project to project depending on where the needs are. As centralized craft excellence scales up, these resources tend to grow to suit the size and needs of the project portfolio, and can also be thought of as a main internal full-time group, whose numbers are occasionally bolstered by contractors and external co-dev resources.

As the CCE team moves across more projects, they continue to gain experience and expertise in ramping on and off various different engines and technologies, and as such become highly valuable in their ability to make an immediate impact.

A CCE can operate at all three of these levels, or potentially just at the high-level, or just at the high and mid-level, the full high-, mid-, and low-level CCE representing a full-spectrum approach of a very large team. If a central team is operating only at the low level, or only at the low and mid-levels, then it becomes an internal resourcing model, rather than a full centre of excellence, as it does not have the overall mandate or accountability for quality across all of the projects. In this case, the overall responsibility for quality becomes decentralized to lie with each audio director at each studio, and as a result may be inconsistent, with one audio director having very different evaluation lenses, best practices, and approaches to the next.

CCEs will also typically work across projects to improve efficiencies by bringing together general overall technology approaches, like shared and centralized third-wave tools and processes that can be used by each studio on each project, and at this point these CCEs will develop a technology branch whose role it is to further develop and generalize specific tools that might have been developed for one particular project and make them available to all, such as a dialogue database, or any velocity-improving procedural tagging and mark-up systems.

Shared expertise with production practices, such as time allotted for mixing after the Gold Master Candidate disc milestone, and having audio teams work on the mix for the patch, may also be propagated throughout the various studios via a CCE.

Overall quality, overall efficiency, technology, best practices, and standards tend to be the accountability of any studio-level audio director or head.

15 What Matters the Most?

In the end, an audio director must be a flexible being, ready to transform into different personalities at different times, to shape-shift as required, without losing a core identity. In game development, nothing can be fixed, everything must have a dynamic design, and everything must be able to flow into different forms and traverse the lines and challenges of the project, both internally (from within the project itself) and externally, from outside of the project on the team and in the game development environment.

This flexibility often results in actively reducing the amount of things you are responsible for, and instead becoming accountable for overall areas. Practically speaking, audio direction must provide a controlled and reliable, expression of the game's story, world and gameplay, the *experience*. This is expressed through the use of the four food groups of sound together as a coordinated expression; sound, music, voice, and mix, all creatively balanced and used to bring the experience to life. The design of each of those food groups, particularly the main content food groups, may answer the game's many briefs in different ways; however, the mix itself answers the final brief, which is the expression of the entirety of the experience. This requires only one thing of the director, which is a deep understanding of the game itself, achieved through nurturing and growing a vision. Being able to answer and decode 'why' about every single element and feature that is requested to make some kind of sound – understanding why anything needs sonification at all, is fundamentally where the process of audio direction leads us.

An audio director needs to understand both the top adventure-line of what is happening onscreen, as well as the subtext (the emotional truth of each moment in the game) of what is happening underneath. Designing sound as part of the team, 'from the inside out' here is crucial, and is a process of being involved and included in the iterative process of discovery that a game team goes through as it refines and sculpts their ideas, removing the features and ideas that do not support the core ideas.

It is only by going through this journey on each project, by travelling along with the team, and discovering things about the game together, that this kind of deeper knowing even becomes possible. As a director, you need to be there

DOI: 10.4324/9781003748465-16

as part of that exploration, offering your own interpretations and ideas along the way, which may either push or pull the experience onscreen towards or away from certain paths. Joining a project at the end will only really allow you to design from the 'outside in', meaning simply, that you are able to embellish and decorate the finished game with sound or music, but not be able to intuitively understand what is 'right' for the particular project, or be able to confidently articulate and know 'why'.

Whoever you are, and however you do it, the audio direction style and personality that you bring to a project is specifically something only you can do in the particular way that you do it. It can feel like you are continually under pressure to be more, do more, and achieve more in the field of audio for games, and this is why I feel it is important to identify the core areas a director must not lose control of and to delegate the rest; no matter what pressure you may feel from yourself or your peers, doing what is best for yourself and the project is your foundation as a director.

The broadest work experiences you can probably gather are to work in many different ways, on many different projects, at many different studios, and try to encounter as many different varieties and responses to the needs of audio direction as you can. This way, you will have developed more archetypes to fall back on, as well as the knowledge that whatever current role you have will be fluid and will need to adapt itself to meet the shape and requirements of each project.

In the end, however you do it, these are perhaps the only outcomes that matter…

The game sounds good.

The team is proud of the results.

The other disciplines are excited about working with you and your team on the next thing.

Index